ABOUT THE

Roberta Morrell is from West Bromwich in the West Midlands. After initially training at the Birmingham School of Music, she studied singing and clarinet at the Royal College of Music in London, before joining the D'Oyly Carte Opera Company in 1972, spending ten years with the famous Gilbert and Sullivan company as both chorister and principal. Thereafter, she has pursued a successful career as a freelance performer and Stage Director, staging over a hundred shows for professional and amateur companies in the UK and North America. She regularly travels to the USA to give Master Classes in vocal presentation and stage technique, her destinations including New York, Boston, Philadelphia, Chicago and Houston. She is the Honorary President of the Gilbert and Sullivan Society of New York. *D'Oyly Carte: Inside Out* is Roberta's fourth G&S-related book and follows *D'Oyly Carte: The Inside Story* and *Kenneth Sandford, Lord High Everything Else*, a biography of the great D'Oyly Carte baritone. Her novel, *Vengeance Dire*, is a murder mystery about an amateur theatre group performing '*The Pirates of Penzance*'. She lives on the beautiful Lleyn Peninsula in North Wales, which provides a peaceful setting for her writing and she is currently working on a second novel, this one set around '*The Mikado*'. When not working, her favourite pastime is holidaying in Spain.

ROBERTA MORRELL

D'Oyly Carte

Inside Out

Matador
9 Priory Business Park,
Wistow Road, Kibworth Beauchamp,
Leicestershire. LE8 0RX
Tel: 0116 279 2299
Email: books@troubador.co.uk
Web: www.troubador.co.uk/matador
Twitter: @matadorbooks

ISBN 978 1838594 817

British Library Cataloguing in Publication Data.
A catalogue record for this book is available from the British Library.

Printed and bound in the UK by TJ International, Padstow, Cornwall
Typeset in 11pt Palatino by Troubador Publishing Ltd, Leicester, UK

Matador is an imprint of Troubador Publishing Ltd

ACKNOWLEDGEMENTS

I wish to thank my D'Oyly Carte colleagues for their co-operation in providing so much of the material for this book and for their unflagging support of my quest to keep alive the legacy of the D'Oyly Carte Opera Company. In particular, I am indebted to Cynthia Morey and Peter Riley, who have never seemed to tire of my many requests for information. I could not have done this without them. Likewise, I acknowledge the generosity and talent of my friend, the great American cartoonist, Arnold Roth, in providing the wonderful images for this book. Thanks, also, are due to The Gilbert and Sullivan Society for its sponsorship and encouragement during the preparation of this book. Its help in promoting my writings about the D'Oyly Carte is invaluable.

FOREWORD

I am delighted to write the foreword to this excellent book by Roberta Morrell.

The D'Oyly Carte Opera Company was the unrivalled champion of Gilbert and Sullivan for over a century, touching and inspiring audiences across the English-speaking world. Sullivan is the most successful light opera composer that Great Britain has produced, and Gilbert has been credited with establishing the director's role in modern theatre, apart from being an excellent lyricist and playwright. Their legacy has delighted since 1875 and is still exciting audiences around the world.

Now, nearly forty years after the company finally closed its doors in 1982, there is very little left to remind us of this unique British institution and the significant contribution it made to the world of professional theatre across the UK, North America and Australasia.

Roberta has been a dear friend and colleague from the very beginning of the International Gilbert and Sullivan Festival, founded by my father, Ian G. Smith, and I. Her intimate knowledge of both the D'Oyly Carte Opera Company and Gilbert and Sullivan made her the ideal choice to direct our first festival production in 1994 and again the following year when the National G & S Opera Company was formed.

Fortunately for us, Roberta has kept a meticulous diary of her time with the company and, in later years, has interviewed many of her colleagues in order to record the amazing stories they have to tell. This book, 'D'Oyly Carte: Inside Out', is a welcome sequel to her first book, 'D'Oyly Carte: The Inside Story' and is, once more, jam-packed with information and anecdotes which any G & S fan will want to read.

Neil G. Smith

INTRODUCTION

The historic D'Oyly Carte Opera Company was a unique theatrical organisation and, in my previous book about this iconic repertory company, *D'Oyly Carte: The Inside Story*, I explored the working life of its various departments between 1950 and its closure in 1982. Bringing the Savoy Operas of W.S. Gilbert and Sir Arthur Sullivan to audiences both at home and abroad for forty-eight weeks of every year for over a century, the D'Oyly Carte was a complex structure, its touring operation necessarily complicated. From the earliest days, under the leadership of its founder, the Victorian impresario, Richard D'Oyly Carte, the company produced many colourful characters, both on the stage and behind the scenes, many of whom were represented in my earlier work. This time around, I have included more recollections, photographs, documents and anecdotes of its performers from the 1950s onwards which, I hope, will add to the understanding of a company the like of which will never be seen again.

The sum of its many parts, the D'Oyly Carte was self-sufficient and doggedly independent to the end of its life, its management determined to continue operating as it had always done. For the performers and staff, outside influences were, from the company's earliest days, a fact of daily life. Here, I have presented examples of some of these external pressures, such as the impact of touring on family life, the dreaded press reviews and the ever-attentive company followers, to give a wider picture of the hardships and pleasures of life on the road. In the twenty-first century, large-scale touring theatre companies are a rarity, the cost of taking more than one show out to the provinces being prohibitive and the lifestyle of performers on tour very different from the days of the D'Oyly Carte. It is, therefore, vitally important to preserve for theatrical posterity the days of low-tech touring; performing a different show every night all year round; theatre digs where the landlady ruled and Sundays when a day off often meant travelling by rail, or in an old car, to the next date on the tour. I hope this book goes some way to achieving this aim.

The works of Gilbert and Sullivan may have a timeless attraction, the satire of W.S. Gilbert often as relevant today as in Victorian times, but we cannot be complacent. Introducing young people to the delights of G&S is essential if the Savoy Operas, as they are also known, with their historical roots at London's Savoy Theatre, are not to become a thing of the dim past. In these days of high-tech, screen-based entertainment, it is easy to forget the simple joy of live theatre. Without the amateur theatre movement, very few people, young or old, would ever see, or be able to afford to attend, a live production on the stage. Large-scale, lavish shows in the West End of London, or on Broadway in New York, which may subsequently go out on tour, incur very high seat prices, but G&S does not necessarily need large sums of money thrown at it to be successful. With imagination and an understanding of the genre, these masterpieces can be easily-accessible to all. It is unthinkable that they should become obscure relics of theatrical history. The original D'Oyly Carte Opera Company may have gone forever, but its legacy deserves to be preserved and I will always strive to perpetuate its importance to British theatre.

Roberta Morrell

CHAPTER ONE

BLOOD, SWEAT AND TEARS

At first sight, life with the D'Oyly Carte Opera Company may well have seemed glamorous and exciting, with appearances at famous theatres and the prospect of overseas tours, but the rigours of life 'on the road' were not to be underestimated. With the exception of the London management based at Savoy Hill, every employee, from the company's greatest stars down to the props man, faced the same challenges arising from a life lived away from home for forty-eight weeks of every year. From the never-ending problem of finding somewhere to stay in over twenty different towns and cities on each tour, to getting laundry done and learning to deal with separation from family, it was a hard life and not one for the faint of heart.

On top of having to deal with such difficulties was the daunting prospect of being contracted to give up to eight performances a week. For the chorus, it was always eight shows, with a couple of rehearsals thrown in for good measure; principals, on average, were 'on' four or five times a week. The strain on their voices from so much singing, or sometimes having to perform with a cold or other illness, never of concern to the management as long as they appeared. Then there were the regular long journeys from one tour date to another on a Sunday, their day off. Until the 1960s, the company was transported as a unit, with performers, backstage staff and management on one specially-hired train, alongside all scenery, costumes and props. No wonder, after so many years of such regimented transport, that most D'Oyly Carters seized the opportunity to buy modest cars to get them from town A to town B. If they were lucky, they might even be able to get home for twenty-four hours.

From the earliest days of the company in the 1870s, wages were low. The D'Oyly Carte was a family-run business for some ninety years, receiving no public funding, so anyone not good at managing money would struggle to cover the cost of accommodation, food, transport, make-up and other essential theatre supplies. And not forgetting that some had to support a family, too. Only in the annual London season was there the opportunity to stay in one place for three months. For those who lived in the capital, it was a chance to save money, but for the rest, they were still away from home. By the mid-1970s, the Actor's Union, Equity, insisted that a weekly touring allowance must be added to salaries to help with necessary living expenses, but even then, there was never much left over. All in all, it was a tough way to make a living, but it was a job offering guaranteed work for a year and that was rare in the theatre world. The D'Oyly Carte always had an endless supply of potential employees anxious to fill the vacancies left by singers who sought a fresh career challenge, or those unable to face another year of touring. Auditions for both principals and chorus were always well-attended.

This extremely challenging lifestyle engendered a special camaraderie between the company members which served to fill the void left by being away from loved ones. The D'Oyly Carte was a family from necessity, but that feeling of belonging remains to this day. It is unlikely that any other company has performers going back to the 1950s who still consider their former colleagues to be 'family'. As the saying goes, 'Once a D'Oyly Carter, always a D'Oyly Carter'. Good times were shared, particularly during lengthy tours of North America. Sight-seeing, parties, the cinema, shopping trips and generous hospitality all helped to keep sane a group of professional performers who rarely went home. Great fun, yes very often, but at a cost.

And what of those left at home? Through no fault of their own, the families of those away for weeks on end suffered a different kind of loneliness. For them, there were not the distractions of D'Oyly Carte life to keep them going, just the responsibility of looking after a home and, sometimes children, single-handed. These Gilbert and Sullivan widows, for so they may well have been, and their children, applied even more pressure to jobbing performers earning a living as best they could under very difficult circumstances.

Mandy Parkin, daughter of Kenneth Sandford, remembers all too well having a father she never really got to know. When Ken joined the D'Oyly Carte in 1957, she was just a toddler, so hardly noticed that her dad was absent most of the time. But, as she grew, she became aware that she only saw him at weekends and even then not every weekend if the company was on tour too far away for him to make the journey to London and back within forty-eight hours. Even worse were the lengthy North American tours when she did not see him for five or six months. She barely remembers travelling to New York with her mother and brother, Anthony, to spend two weeks' holiday with him in 1962, but it was a rare opportunity for the family to spend time together.

Mandy recalls that the annual three-month London season was not much better. By the time she came home from school, her dad was getting ready to leave for the evening performance and she and Anthony were in bed by the time he came home. On Sundays, he was expected to be the father he could not be for the rest of the week, but he also had a list of household chores that needed doing, so the amount of time he could devote to his children was limited and Mandy recalls that he was often tired and, sometimes, irritated by the demands of two young children. She describes him as a rather stern and strict father, with whom she and her brother could rarely have fun. Only during week-long runs of *The Pirates of Penzance* and *HMS Pinafore*, in which Ken did not appear, was there the chance to see a more relaxed side of her father. She once remarked to me that she found it difficult to understand how two very conservative parents could have produced such a bohemian daughter. I told her that her father, as known to his D'Oyly Carte colleagues, was a man with a great, if sometimes juvenile, sense of humour, who could easily be described as a 'closet bohemian'. This revelation gave Mandy great pleasure, but it is indicative of the problems of the D'Oyly Carte lifestyle that a child knew so little of her father's real character.

For Ken's wife, Pauline, was the hardship of raising two children almost single-handed. She admits that, although she was very proud of Ken's success, she came to hate the D'Oyly Carte Opera Company, bitterly resenting the impact it had on her life, with the loneliness and responsibility she had to endure during the long tours. She also told me that when Ken was at home, she expected him to make up for being away so much. This may seem harsh, but how many other D'Oyly Carte wives felt the same? Surely, a perfectly understandable reaction to the months of enforced separation?

On the other side of this difficult situation was a man who also made sacrifices. Providing for his family was always Ken's priority, to the point of giving up all ambition of a career in grand opera, always his cherished dream as a professional singer. Once offered a principal contract at Glyndbourne, he was sorely tempted, but it was only for six months, so how would he manage for the other half of the year? He declined the offer and that was the story for the rest of his twenty-five-year career with the D'Oyly Carte Opera Company. Much as he enjoyed his work and the challenges he always perceived the Savoy Operas of Gilbert and Sullivan to present, Ken put his family first and personal ambition second, gratefully accepting year-round employment. But that was not the only sacrifice he made. For his children to get good, private education and live in a nice house, he spent a quarter of a century living in digs, constantly travelling and doing without the comforts of a home life. It is unlikely that either party truly understood how hard it was on the other side of the fence. The following brief extract from Ken's diary prior to departure for the 1962 American tour tells us much.

August 9th 1962. I was determined to spend as much time with my family as possible, in spite of the detailed instructions which seemed to make things difficult. It was ordered that baggage should be delivered to the Embankment entrance of the Savoy Hotel by 5.30pm and then we would receive travel documents and dollars from the touring manager. I phoned the office and obtained permission to deposit my effects earlier in the day and to pick up my travel papers at 4pm in order that I might return home and have a little more time with my family before joining the main gathering of the company at 8pm. This all occurred as planned – it was rather fun to see that both Mandy and Anthony made a hit with the Savoy doorkeeper. It not only gave me more time with the children, but also enabled me to give last-minute instructions to Pauline on how to, and how not to, put the car into the garage – something I had promised to do and had not. I have a feeling that the instruction might have been worthwhile.

The experiences of the Sandfords were very likely shared by many a D'Oyly Carter with a family and one wonders how, before the age of the motor car, any of them ever managed to get home. The D'Oyly Carte was a touring company from its beginning in Victorian times, so any married person who joined must surely have realised it was not the job for them if they could not deal with the demands of life on the road away from home for months on end. However, it certainly worked for some. Gordon MacKenzie joined the company as a chorister in 1954, serving three separate stints in that capacity, before becoming Assistant Company Manager in 1969 and Business Manager from 1980 until the company's closure in 1982. A Scotsman whose home was in Greenock, he was married with four children and, apart from the company's annual four-week holiday, he usually managed to get home only once or twice during the course of a tour, with the bonus of staying at home when the company played in Scotland every second year. Yet his marriage survived, although one can only wonder how his wife coped during those twenty-eight years. Principal baritone, Michael Rayner, had five children to support, but at least living in Derby meant he could get home most weekends. It certainly took a special kind of wife and mother to deal with the pressure of raising a family on her own, when a phone call to her absent husband might not be enough to deal with an emergency.

But it was not only married men with children who had family commitments. When John Reed was offered a contract to understudy Peter Pratt as principal comedian in 1951, he had to take into consideration the welfare of his elderly mother before accepting the job. He knew that constantly being away from his Durham home would have a big impact on her life. Although he had two sisters, John took the care of his mum very seriously and they were very close. Having planned her care to the best of his ability, he joined the D'Oyly Carte, but feelings of guilt at leaving her were never far away. Perhaps it was this strong sense of family loyalty that moved John to take Jill Pert under his wing when her beloved grandfather unexpectedly passed away during the company's tour of Australia and New Zealand in 1979. On her first overseas tour, Jill was still coming to terms with her new responsibility as understudy to principal contralto, Patricia Leonard, when she received the bad news. Obviously unable to attend his funeral, Jill was terribly upset, but help was there when she was struggling to cope with her loss.

'The company, especially Reedy and Beti Lloyd-Jones, rallied round and supported me. It was a real example of the "family" that was the D'Oyly Carte.'

During the early stages of the 1978 tour of North America, when the company was playing the O'Keefe Centre in Toronto, Wig Mistress, Heather Perkins, got a message to say that her mother had been taken seriously ill. There was no option for her but to immediately fly back to the UK. This left the company in something of a dilemma, because Heather was solely responsible for the care of the many wigs which required daily maintenance. On hearing this news, principal soprano, Julia Goss, volunteered to step into the breach until Heather returned, an offer gratefully accepted by the touring management. Her own job was demanding enough, so taking on this extra responsibility was a big ask, but she didn't mind, as she explains.

'It was a case of mucking in to help in an emergency. I'd always been good with hair, so I knew I could keep the wigs tidy. Every morning, Peter Riley put out all the wigs needing dressing and I got cracking putting in rollers, curling ringlets and generally smartening them up for the next show. It was easy enough until I got to the Pirate King's huge curly wig – dealing with that was something else!' Julia continued in her temporary job as Wig Mistress for a few weeks until Heather was able to return. If ever there was an example of the 'family' looking out for each other, that was it.

In 1972, Patricia Leonard joined the D'Oyly Carte chorus knowing that she would be leaving the care of her small son, Andrew, to his grandparents. This decision was not taken without much soul-searching, but she knew that the money she would earn with the company meant security for them. As a divorcee, keeping a roof over their heads was the most important thing, but her maternal instinct was strong and regret at abandoning him was always there. Spending time with him at weekends was as much as she could do, but the five-month tours of North America in 1976 and 1978, really hit hard and Trish very much missed her son. When it was announced that the company was to tour Australia and New Zealand in 1979, Trish knew that she could not leave Andrew again for such a long time so soon after the American tour. Drastic action was needed: she would take him with her.

Not quite as simple as it sounded, Trish had many things to organise, not the least being obtaining permission to take him out of school for five months. Andrew's teachers agreed, with the proviso that his education continued while he was away. Chorus tenor and company choreographer, Alan Spencer, a former teacher, kindly volunteered to tutor Andrew in the work provided by Andrew's school. By now playing the principal contralto roles and married to fellow-Carter, Michael Buchan, Trish was able to enjoy the tour Down Under and a family life for all of them. Even then, Andrew's care whilst she and Mike were at the theatre had to be considered, the solution being to use the principals not appearing in the show to look after him. It all worked splendidly and Andrew never seemed to suffer from the less-than-ideal circumstances of his upbringing. Indeed, Drew has gone on to enjoy a successful career on the technical side of the theatre. Obviously in his blood!

During the long history of the D'Oyly Carte, there must have been examples of wives joining the company leaving husbands at home and Pamela 'Mavis' Baxter can be confirmed as one of them. When she accepted a chorus and mezzo-soprano understudy contract in 1979, she and her husband decided that it was an ideal opportunity for them to earn a regular salary, so she worked away and he worked from their London home. It may have seemed an odd arrangement, but it must have suited them, because Pam stayed with the company until its closure in 1982. The popular principal soprano, Jean Hindmarsh, was another. Jean left the company in 1960 and got married that year, but she returned for several guest seasons over the next few years.

There are numerous instances of people meeting and marrying within D'Oyly Carte. Darrell Fancourt and Eleanor Evans; Peter Pratt and Joyce Wright; Donald Adams and Muriel Harding; Alan Styler and Vera Ryan; Alan Barrett and Mary Sansom; Jon Ellison and Joy Mornay, Ralph Mason and Anne Sessions; George Cook and Marian Martin; Norman Wright and Christene Palmer; John Broad and Rosalind Griffiths, Gareth Jones and Vivian Tierney to name but a few. Both Isidore Godfrey and Peter Riley had two D'Oyly Carte wives – Marguerite Kynaston and Ann Drummond-Grant; Abby Hadfield and Yvonne Sommeling respectively. Not all of these couples went on to have children, but of those who did, the women who left the company to raise a family without their husbands, the pressure of solitary responsibility was probably less because they had an understanding of how hard a life it was for their husbands on tour without them. They knew the sacrifices being made by each partner and there was no feeling of abandonment; the couples had made a choice to have a family and accepted the accompanying disadvantages.

Vera Ryan and Alan Styler had three daughters, so life for Vera was not easy after she left the company to raise their family with Alan away on tour, as she relates.

'If you were married to a D'Oyly Carte performer you had to be prepared for separations of forty-eight weeks in the year and six-month tours of the USA and Canada. Of course there were occasional days off, but sometimes the journey would be too impractical for Alan to get home. Helen, our second daughter, was born when Alan was on a Scottish and North East England tour, so she was six weeks old before he saw her. I already had Madeleine, who was just ten and a half months old when Helen was born, so they were both babes in arms. Home was a bungalow in Redditch, miles from anywhere, but I adored bringing up the girls and looked forward to

Alan's days at home. I just wished I could drive, because it would have made life so much easier but, in 1962, women drivers were a rarity.

'I kept a social life going with the help of a good friend who was secretary of the Redditch Music Club, and a local piano teacher and I would get together for sessions when I could have a sing. My next-door neighbour was a wonderful support and even had a connecting alarm bell fitted between our houses in case I went into labour during the night – which I did! In those days, home births were not uncommon and my midwife was a darling. I remember the milkman took the news round the estate that the midwife's car was parked on our drive. One year, my sister, Abigail, who was at university in Manchester, got a summer job nearby and was great company for us during her summer vacation. I did some singing and even managed a summer season at Minehead, taking my father with me to look after the girls when I was at the theatre.

'After the 1962 American tour, Alan became ill and had to have a lung operation. The hospital was in Kent, so I packed up the girls and stayed with my older sister, Mary, who was with the Royal Opera. The journey took me seven hours there and back, but I was able to visit Alan a few times during the two weeks he was in hospital. When I became pregnant with our youngest, Bridget, I put my foot down and told Alan that I was done with being shut away in a small country town. I wanted to move back to Manchester, where I knew I would get a great deal of help from my parents and family. I must admit the goodbyes were awful during Alan's touring days, but it was lovely when he came home – you could just carry on married life as normal and I never agonised over the separations. Taking three girls to school and back and generally bringing them up by myself was good training for the sad time when Alan was no longer with us. The girls were already used to it being just the four of us.

'I joined Alan for the 1966 American tour. The Company Manager, Bert Newby, was determined that I should be part of the company and Bridget D'Oyly Carte was very supportive. My sister, Abigail, was also with the company by then. I hated leaving the girls, but Alan really needed me at that time. I left them with the lady whose flat I had rented for the Minehead season. The girls liked her and she had four children of her own, so they were fine. I left the following spring and slipped back into normal life. Alan wanted to buy a pub as a second career after the Carte. Did he think I was some kind of Amazon who could bring up three children on my own and run a business at the same time while he was away on tour? I know Philip Potter's wife, Gillian, did it and I admired her for it, but there was no way I could. The answer was no.'

Vera Ryan's fascinating insight into the life of a D'Oyly Carte wife clearly demonstrates the impact of touring on family and home life for company employees, but this was only one, albeit one of the biggest, of the pressures which made their gruelling job even more difficult. Problems with health were always dreaded by those on tour. Coughs and colds were common enough. Hot stuffy dressing rooms being the ideal breeding ground for viruses, it was not unusual for a bug to rapidly spread from one singer to another. For choristers, it was possible to hide when suffering from a heavy cold. With eight singers to each chorus line, someone 'marking' (best defined as not using full vocal weight) did not make too much difference. For the principals, however, it was a different matter. Generally speaking, a head cold could be managed, even if tone was a little nasal, but singing with a sore throat, or chest infection, was not only difficult, but also brought risk of damage to vocal cords which could lead to a prolonged absence from performances. It was better to be off for a few nights than a few weeks.

Everyone had their own ideas as to how to avoid getting a cold, with vitamin supplements always a popular choice, but James Conroy-Ward's recommendation for keeping bugs at bay was not exactly user-friendly, as Harold Sharples, who sang as principal tenor for a year from 1979, remembers only too well.

'James, bless him, was a lovely chap to work with, but was always a little concerned about his health – mind you, he had great responsibility with all the famous patter parts to portray. But he did have one rather unendearing habit. If he felt a cold coming on, or was under the weather, he would chew raw cloves of garlic! One particular Saturday, at Sadler's Wells I think it was, we had two performances of *Mikado* ahead. James had munched on some garlic, but Barbara Lilley, who was playing 'Yum-Yum', and I only realised when we came to our first section of dialogue with 'Ko-Ko'. It was then that the eye-watering fumes hit us. Those two shows were really tricky to manage as Barbara and I worked with James whilst trying to keep our heads turned away from him. I swear the air was vibrating around him. Of course, he was threatened with dire consequences if he did it again!'

When away from home, any D'Oyly Carter needing medical attention had the bother of finding a doctor to treat them. The company management, quite reasonably, required proof of any condition which kept them off the stage for more than a few days, but contact details for local surgeries were, usually, available at every theatre. Most conditions were of a minor nature, but it was not unknown for performers to need hospital visits or emergency treatment. However hard they tried to look after themselves, performers inevitably succumbed to illness or accident every now and then. Feeling unwell is bad enough when at home, but pity the poor souls being ill in digs miles away from family. Just another pressure that went with the job.

Problems with teeth were a perennial nightmare for those away from home. Losing a filling was a small matter by comparison with losing a front crown. Apart from looking dreadful on the stage, a large gap in teeth made singing almost impossible, the lisping sound emerging instead of smooth tone invariably led to a principal being off until the crown could be replaced. This meant a dash to find a local dentist prepared to fit them in for an emergency appointment. It was Kenneth Sandford's worst nightmare and, with very few exceptions, the only reason he missed a performance. But there was one memorable exception. A hardy Yorkshireman, Ken was as tough as they came, but he once went on as 'Pooh-Bah' in *The Mikado* when he should have been in his digs with his feet up. A septic big toe giving him considerable pain, he went to Edinburgh Royal Infirmary for treatment, but was not expecting to be given a general anaesthetic in order for the inflamed digit to be lanced. Told by the doctor not to drive for twenty-four hours, he left his car at the hospital and took a bus to the theatre. As no-one had said anything about not working, Ken floated through the performance on a pleasant tide of anaesthesia, admiring his own performance and wishing he could bottle the feeling. How he loved to dine out on that story!

The production of adrenalin associated with performing often got D'Oyly Carters through a show; however bad they felt when the overture was being played, once the curtain was up, they somehow managed to get through unscathed. There was a famous company story that a chorus man, in great pain, went to the toilet, passed a large kidney stone and went straight back on the stage to complete the show. Such dedication was admirable, but most ailments were managed with professionalism and performers did not go off unless it was absolutely unavoidable.

One of my happiest memories is an incident which spawned a long-running tradition between John Ayldon and myself. One day, for a reason I cannot now remember, I accepted a lift from baritone, John Broad. Unfortunately, I rather carelessly left my thumb in his car door when I shut it. A visit to hospital revealed a severe sprain which needed a firm dressing to support the joint. The performance that evening was *The Yeomen of the Guard*, during which I did my best to keep my oversized thumb out of view. However, in the second act finale, the ladies were required to have their hands folded at the waist. Even though John Ayldon, playing 'Sergeant Meryll', was on the opposite side of the stage to me, he spotted my involuntary 'thumbs up' and, for some reason, found it hilarious. From that day onwards, not one performance of *Yeomen* passed when John and I did not exchange a subtle thumbs up across the stage during the tragic events unfolding at the end of the show. Neither of us ever forgot.

Minor illnesses, strains and sprains were managed easily enough, but anything more serious could be a nightmare for both performers and management, particularly on overseas tours, when visits to doctors, dentists and hospitals would involve complicated claims on the company's medical insurance. Ken Robertson-Scott, who was Stage Manager on the 1978 tour of North America, can remember an insurance claim being made on his behalf when he broke his wrist during the madcap antics of the infamous D'Oyly Carte Olympics at Saratoga Springs, when several injuries occurred during an impromptu sports day. The day after he had taken a heavy fall during the tug o' war across the swimming pool, he was at work setting up for *Iolanthe*, when someone suggested his wrist should be checked, even though he was not in too much pain. Ken's boss, Peter Riley and his wife, Yvonne

Sommeling, drove him to the local hospital, where an x-ray revealed a break and his wrist was put in a cast during the chaos of a major incident in the Emergency Room. Although he managed at work without too much difficulty, doing his laundry was another matter. With very little opportunity to have access to a washing machine, D'Oyly Carters had to wash clothes in their hotel bathrooms, but Ken could not do this with his arm in plaster. Julia Goss, whom he describes as 'like an older sister', took pity on him and did his washing, as well as her own, taking it back to him on coat hangers to dry in his room. He has never forgotten her kindness.

After the company got back to the UK, Ken remembers getting lots of requests for information about his injury from the insurance company handling his claim in America but, worse still, he was not happy about his wrist. A visit to an orthopaedic consultant in his native North East led to the wrist having to be broken again and re-set, because the American hospital had made such a mess of it. This meant several more weeks of difficulty working in a plaster cast. And all because some of the company members decided to hold a sports day to pass the time on their day off, but he would not have missed such a memorable event for the world.

Although seeking medical advice was sometimes essential, company members would try to avoid this inconvenience, if possible. During the 1976 season in New York, John Reed was ill with a mystery ailment and unable to perform for several days, but he refused to seek medical attention, determined he would soon be better. I can remember taking food to his hotel room, where I found him looking dishevelled and weak, but he was adamant he did not want to see a doctor. Why the company management did not insist on him taking medical advice has not been possible to discover. It was a prestigious season and audiences would have been disappointed by his non-appearance, but he did recover sufficiently to complete the New York run. John was seldom off, but his enormous popularity with audiences put him under pressure to appear even when feeling unwell, so it seems odd that, on this occasion, he chose not to see a doctor to help speed his recovery.

Although the D'Oyly Carte management, quite naturally, expected its employees to look after their health, there were occasions when very serious illness struck down performers. It was at these times that a caring side was shown by the Savoy Hill management in London, which so often seemed to be far-removed from the lengthy tours in the provinces. There are numerous instances of singers being referred for specialist care at the expense of the company. One might argue that it was in the interest of the company to keep its performers, particularly the principals, in good health but, in fairness, there was a genuine desire to help. Bridget D'Oyly Carte, who was usually seen by the performers out on tour as a remote figure living in splendid isolation in the Savoy Hotel, took a keen interest in the welfare of those suffering from serious conditions. Known to have personally paid for treatment and recuperation holidays, she kept in touch with the progress of such leading artists as Alan Styler, Ann Drummond-Grant, Michael Rayner, Mary Sansom and John Webley during their periods of ill-health. Jobs were kept open and wages paid for as long as necessary; loyalty was shown to those in need, the soft underbelly of a hard-nosed management there for all to see.

In the early 1970s, soprano, Rosalind Griffiths, benefited from the kindness of the management when she suffered persistent bouts of acute tonsillitis. At the company's expense, she was sent for a consultation with one of the country's leading specialists, when she was told she needed an immediate tonsillectomy. Within a very short time, the company had paid for the operation at a private hospital, where some of the company came to visit her. She remembers chorus baritone, Jason Shute, bringing her strawberries which the nurses ate. Ros has always been grateful for the care the D'Oyly Carte's General Manager, Frederic Lloyd, showed her when she was so ill. It was a horrible time, but an amusing incident stayed with her long after the pain had gone. She and her husband, John Broad, laugh about it to this day.

'John and I were staying on the caravan site at Crystal Palace during the winter season at Sadler's Wells Theatre. I was feeling dreadful, but John and the other Carte folk staying on the site went off for the show, leaving me tucked up at home. Our little caravan boasted a small gas fire, which kept the place cosy, so I settled down for the evening. When the pain in my throat got really bad, I turned to my trusted cure to ease the discomfort – three teaspoons of hot piccalilli followed by a couple of wine gums. Sounds weird, but it worked. A bit later on, I needed to go to the loo, so I hurried across to the toilet block but, when I got back to the caravan, I had somehow managed to lock myself out. I was so cross, but all I could do was look longingly through the window at the cosy fire and the piccalilli and wine gums on the table. It was a cold night and I was freezing in just my pyjamas and dressing gown, so I went to the site office, where the guy on duty rang the theatre to get a message to John, then fed me tea and biscuits until John could get back to rescue me. Needless to say, he called me a few choice names as he produced the caravan keys!'

Of course, there is always the exception to prove the rule and Christene Palmer was rather less than impressed by the lack of concern shown to her when she was struck down with flu.

'I think it was the 1968 American tour. We had been playing in Denver when I came down with a nasty Asian flu virus and I was too poorly to fly to Los Angeles with the rest of the company. I was left to fend for myself and John Reed arranged for me to stay with friends of his in Central City, who looked after me with great kindness until I was well enough to fly to Los Angeles. I think the touring management must have seen this as a great inconvenience. Not only did my understudy have to go on for a week, but a flight had to be specially arranged for me. I remember walking into the theatre in LA and saw the company manager, Bert Newby. No sympathy, no asking if I was feeling better, just "Good job you're back". In New York, the impresario, Sol Hurok, would not have understudies on, so I had to do every performance. It was very tough; you had to look after yourself to get through eight shows a week and it was easy to get run down and exhausted.'

It was not always the management who could be unsympathetic. Christene's husband, Norman Wilfred Wright, was feeling light-headed and dizzy during a season in Newcastle-Upon-Tyne. Wondering if the problem was with his ears, he went to see a doctor, who examined them and sarcastically asked him if he was in the right job!

There is no doubt that inevitable dealings with the D'Oyly Carte management could bring pressure to performers whose lives on tour gave them enough stress. Although year-round job security was one of the attractions of working for the company, it was not guaranteed, because contracts were not automatically renewed and that was always a worry. Principals wishing to stay with the company faced an interview with Frederic Lloyd in which they set out their salary demands, followed by an anxious wait for the arrival of a formal offer for the following season. For the big names, their interviews usually involved wrangling with Mr Lloyd for a salary increase which they believed befitted their importance to the company. But Lloyd was a wily negotiator and invariably got the best of the bargain. Christene Palmer remembers once getting an invitation to lunch at the Savoy for her annual review. It set alarm bells ringing as she realised that the General Manager would wine and dine her in order to get the best deal he could from her. She knew she would have to be on her mettle if he wasn't to run rings around her – but he did.

The quality of the work of the principals was easy to assess given that they appeared several times every week, but not so for choristers embedded within a large group of voices. The company addressed this matter of quality control by periodically holding what were known as 'field days', during which all chorus members had to sing for their job. There was no privacy, as one singer after another went onto the stage in the hearing of all the others waiting in the wings; it was not a pleasant experience. Failure to be offered a new contract following assessment was uncommon, but not unknown. When the long-serving tenor, William Palmerley, was told his contract was not being renewed after one field day, there was huge sympathy for him while he was obliged to see out the remainder of his contract. On the other hand, a field day was an opportunity to impress in the hope of gaining small parts and understudies, but every chorus member was glad when it was over.

Known pressures, whether from within or without, were a fact of D'Oyly Carte life which had to be taken in stride, but Peggy Ann Jones was staggered when she received a summons to jury service. She contacted the relevant court officials to explain the nature of her job, but got nowhere so, in desperation, asked Frederic Lloyd to plead her case. Of course, this smooth operator somehow managed to get her excused, but he couldn't resist the opportunity for a little tongue-in-cheek fun when he wrote to inform her he would intercede on her behalf.

28th May, 1969.

Dear Miss Jones,

Thank you for sending me all the jury papers which I now return, with the exception of the postcard which I have sent on to the Undersheriff.

I h ve discussed this matter with Equity, who tell me that actors (even touring actors) are not exempt from jury duty but, as you will see from the enclosed copy, I have written a covering letter to the Undersheriff in the hope that they will release you from duty.

If not, the only thing to do will be to hope and pray that the Court rises before 5 each day and that there is nothing between Hertford and Wimbledon to prevent you belting down the road to arrive in time; perhaps they wouldn't object to your sitting in the jury box in your evening's costume and make-up ! However, I hope we shall be able to get you released.

Yours sincerely,

[signature]

General Manager.

Miss P. A. Jones,
The D'Oyly Carte Opera Company,
A.B.C.,
Peterborough,
Northants.

P.S. - We'll have you in Trial next !

DIRECTORS : BRIDGET D'OYLY CARTE · HUGH WONTNER, M.V.O. · MARTIN. B. RADCLIFFE · F. C. SAWFORD

Peggy can also attest to a very different kind of problem she had to face. If a principal is not happy with the costume they are expected to wear, it can affect confidence in their performance. When her 'Mad Margaret' costume for *Ruddigore* was redesigned in 1964, she was very disappointed by its plainness, which she felt unsuited to the character. But worse than that, the skirt was split to the top of the thigh, which Peggy thought would be very revealing when getting up and down from the floor. Extremely worried by this, she wrote to the company owner, Bridget D'Oyly Carte, to express her concerns. So funny did she find the ensuing letters from Miss Carte, that she has kept them for whenever she feels in need of a giggle.

BRIDGET D'OYLY CARTE LIMITED

Telegrams : Savoyard, London   1, SAVOY HILL, LONDON, W.C.2   Telephone : Temple Bar 1533

14th August, 1964.

Dear Miss Jones,

    I am sorry I missed you this morning, as I was held up in
a meeting, and to hear that you are worried about your new split
skirt.

    I will arrange for Mrs. Keating to have a special pair of
knickers made for you — ragged and long, which should meet your
problem.

    I don't wish to have the skirt altered at all until I have
had an opportunity to see the whole costume in action on the stage.
I will arrange to do this as soon as possible. Mr. Goffin will be up in
Wolverhampton and I have told him to discuss the matter with you, and he
will see if the knickers are the answer, and if it is necessary to alter
the skirt.

               Yours sincerely,

Miss Peggy Ann Jones,
88A, Main Street,
Balderton,
Newark,
Notts.

DIRECTORS: BRIDGET D'OYLY CARTE · HUGH WONTNER, M.V.O. · A. F. MOIR · F. C. SAWFORD

18

1 SAVOY HILL · LONDON · W·C·2

TEMPLE BAR 1533

October 9th
1914

Dear Miss Jones,

I thought your new costume was a great success and certainly seems to have inspired you! I have never seen a better performance of Mad Margaret than at all you gave last evening.

The whole show went well I thought & I hope will be a great success in America.

Yours sincerely
Sara...

19

Letters from the management rarely contained good news and often involved a reprimand. Norman Wilfred Wright remembers a member of the men's chorus, who will remain nameless, got rather cross that one of the other men had picked up his *Iolanthe* coronet by mistake. Finding the exchanged headgear did not fit properly, it was unceremoniously slung into the wings in disgust. This incident, having been noticed by the Stage Manager, was reported and led to a letter of admonishment from General Manager, Frederic Lloyd, which Norman was shown. It contained the typically Lloydian comment, 'The peers in the House of Lords didn't do that sort of thing.'

Such quirkiness from the upper echelons of the company may have been amusing, but there were times when the hard side of their business dealings became clear. When Harold 'Harry' Sharples joined the company as a replacement for principal tenor, Geoffrey Shovelton, in 1980, it was his dream job. But little did he know when he signed his contract that it would be his first and last. After a year on tour, when he thoroughly enjoyed both his work and the company of his new colleagues, he was told his contract would not be renewed. Shocked, angry and hurt, he could think of no reason he should be sacked. His reviews had been favourable and audience reaction good, so why was he being dismissed? He tried in vain to get an explanation from the General Manager, but all he got was a letter to say how personally sorry Mr Lloyd was that he would not be staying with the company. It was some time later that Harry heard something about this matter which left him dumbfounded. As he understands it, when Geoffrey Shovelton, tired of constant touring, left in 1979, he was told that he could have his job back at any time. After what turned out to be a break of a year, Geoff decided he wanted to rejoin the company, which left Harry surplus to requirements and that was that. It is interesting that the Company Manager at the time, Peter Riley, thinks it unlikely that Harry would have been engaged on that basis and that he was unaware that Geoff had any agreed sabbatical. He thinks it more likely that someone on the music or production staff thought that Harry had been the wrong choice, so Geoff was approached on that basis and agreed to return.

'I cannot remember any staff meetings at which I was present when it was decided that Harry should not have his contract renewed. On the other hand, I was not party to any possible correspondence between the music and production departments and Savoy Hill. There may be something relevant in the archives.'

Either way, Harry will never know the real truth, but his year with the D'Oyly Carte certainly did not turn out as he would have wished. Although he got on well with his colleagues and loved the roles he played, there was a large fly in the ointment, the Director of Productions, Leonard Osborn. From the word go, Osborn took Harry to task on the way he played his roles, particularly 'Colonel Fairfax' in *The Yeomen of the Guard*, constantly criticising his characterisation and delivery of dialogue. As a professional, he did his best to do as asked, but it was never good enough. Harry makes it quite clear that he believes Leonard Osborn deliberately tried to undermine him. He recalls several occasions when Osborn asked him to say his lines in a certain way, which he dutifully did, only to be told to deliver them in a way that he had already been told was wrong. Having become utterly frustrated, he confronted Osborn, telling him in no uncertain terms that he was going to play the roles in his own way and not the way Leonard Osborn had played them.

It could be argued that this clash with the Director of Productions might have been the reason for Harry's dismissal, had he been the only one to experience such treatment. Another principal tenor to come in for the 'Osborn treatment' was Meston Reid, along with patter man, James Conroy-Ward and principal soprano, Evette Davis, all of whom felt that his constant criticism of their work did little for their confidence. Evette's D'Oyly Carte career, like that of Harry Sharples, lasted for just one year and Harry recalls Mr Osborn pulling he and Evette from a rehearsal in Norwich and tearing them to shreds for their performances as 'Casilda' and 'Luiz' in *The Gondoliers*. Both Meston and James did excellent impersonations of Osborn's aloof, nose-in-the-air manner, much to the amusement of their colleagues. Somehow, sending him up seemed to take the sting out of their suffering.

That principal performers had to deal with such pressure when their job was difficult enough seems unthinkable but, in fairness, what went on between Leonard Osborn and some of those in his artistic charge may never have been known at Savoy Hill.

Given that life on tour with the D'Oyly Carte Opera Company was so fraught with hardships, one may well wonder why anyone would choose to earn a living in this way. Yes, it was regular work in a world where finding employment was never easy, but there was more to it than that. Professional opera singers have a need to perform to an audience, to gain experience and to further their careers. The D'Oyly Carte gave that and more. It provided the opportunity for principals to become proficient in the art of performing and developing roles over a long period of time as no other company could. For the chorus, too, was the chance to prove their worth and to gain promotion within the company. If it was not the easiest job in the world, there was always the strong family unit providing companionship and support when the going got tough.

CHAPTER TWO

MEET THE PRESS

A very different kind of pressure with which the principals of the D'Oyly Carte were faced was the impact of newspaper coverage on their lives. Having to deal with press reviews was no small matter, bringing pleasure or pain to performers striving to do their best on a daily basis. From the management point of view, good press early in a season was essential to help fill any empty seats, whilst bad press was likely to have the opposite effect.

The calibre of theatre critics reviewing a show has always been something of a lottery, because many of them do not have the relevant ability of the artists they critique, surely the ideal situation if their opinions are to be respected? Most trades and professions require formal qualifications, but not so for a journalist specialising in reviewing a variety of live theatrical performances. However well they may know the show they are paid to review, most give an opinion based solely on personal like or dislike of the presentation they see. Many, particularly those working for small provincial newspapers, know little about the techniques of dancing, singing or acting and certainly could not demonstrate how to do it better than the performers they criticise. If they are unschooled in hard-earned stage and musical skills, how are they qualified to make fair and objective comment? A critique, therefore, is a subjective viewpoint and what one reviewer enjoys about a performance, another might hate. Understandably, this has always been a bone of contention for performers in the firing line.

Most of us have seen a show we thoroughly enjoyed, only to read a damning review of it the next day, leaving us to wonder if the person who had written the report had been at the same performance. The cynical view amongst most performers is that a reviewer could be a local sports reporter drafted in to cover a show, who reads the programme in the bar before cobbling together a precis of the plot and list of the characters, then submitting it as a critique. There was once an instance of a D'Oyly Carte principal being given a bad review, when it was actually their understudy performing, suggesting that the reviewer was not in the theatre at the beginning of the show when the cast change would have been announced. Yet that hack's words could have carried weight with anyone thinking about going to see the show and have an adverse effect on the reputation of the unfairly-maligned leading performer. Of course, it must be said that there have always been well-respected critics thoroughly versed in the subjects on which they make judgement, but they are not a common breed. There are also those who revel in holding a reputation for scything criticism, their biting, occasionally witty, decimation of a performer, or show, making for good reading even though their harsh words may be unjustified. In North America, caustic reviews of both D'Oyly Carte performers and performances were not uncommon, as the following extracts show.

THE TORONTO DAILY STAR, JANUARY 2ND, 1962

Gillian Knight, the contralto who sings all of Gilbert's ugly old lady roles (last night she was the Queen of the Fairies) has adopted a uniform vocal style and personality for all her parts. It is the highly artificial style – foggy-edged timbre, eccentric character – made familiar by countless church basement productions of G&S.

Michael Rayner seemed strained and miscast in the mock-romantic baritonal bravado of Captain Corcoran, and he looked considerably, illogically, older than his quasi-twin, Ralph Rackstraw. In that role, Meston Reid again capitalized on an aura of long-legged, boyish innocence, but his tight tenor creaked or squeaked in just about every climatic ascent. John Ayldon's authoritative Dick Deadeye suffered from bland amiability, and Lyndsie Holland contributed a vocally unsteady, unwieldy Little Buttercup.

Last night the D'Oyly Carte Opera Company of London presented "The Gondoliers" at the O'Keefe Centre. Even if Toronto audiences did not have last summer's excellent Stratford version of this Gilbert and Sullivan opera as a standard of comparison the performance could only be ranked as dreadful. The debacle was partly the result of poor singing, weak acting, static and unimaginative staging, timid and capricious conducting, lack-lustre orchestral playing, a mumbling, frozen chorus, amateurish dancing, colourless costumes, old-fashioned sets and irrational lighting. The remainder of the blame lies with the inhuman schedule set by impresario, Sol Hurok. Last night's performance was the company's fifth in 48 hours. Five of the soloists sang major roles in every one of these performances. It's a wonder they could stumble on stage, let alone act or sing.

The biggest fault of all, however, is in George Foa's staging. Foa has broken the Gilbertian mould slightly, but has apparently not bothered to invent action to keep the stage interesting during the many dull spots in Gilbert's book. For that matter, even Gilbert's best moments are hardly utilised.

Cuba, Rome and Greece have been joined by the D'Oyly Carte. The dismal news this morning is that the greatest Gilbert and Sullivan company of the lot has gone to pot. Last night's performance of "The

Mikado" was utterly miserable. Everything about the overture was all wrong and when the principals came on, matters were worse. These players have a certain ability to sing (a fair novelty) but in the style of a genial shire's volunteer choral society. This talent was confused by, I hope, conductor Godfrey's unfamiliar musicians, but worse than that, it was hopelessly uninspired, bored. To be bored by "Mr. President" is one thing, but to be bored by something infinitely wittier, more timely (despite its 77 years) is unforgivable.

THE CHICAGO DAILY TRIBUNE, DECEMBER 20TH, 1962

Not too much can be said for the return of the D'Oyly Carters in "The Mikado", which launched a brief engagement in the Civic Opera House Tuesday night. John Reed's Ko-Ko and Kenneth Sandford's Pooh-Bah came closest to the point in a troupe badly in need of a director with authority and a style with spine. Aside from Donald Adams, the Mikado of older days, most of the others seem incurably provincial. Thomas Round is no Nanki-Poo even when he finds the pitch, Jennifer Toye's amplified "The Moon and I" is torture to the unprotected ear and Gillian Knight's Katisha is rather like a caricature of Turandot – which is not such a bad idea.

Herbert Whittaker, reviewing *The Mikado* for the *Toronto Globe* in 1968, launched such a scathing attack on John Reed that it is worth reproducing the whole piece, which he headlined: *Bad case of mime in good Mikado.*

Last night, I was favored by the company of two of the New Savoyards Junior Division. They were in the happy state of loving The Mikado from recordings and were now seeing that remarkably happy creation in the flesh. "It's too funny" was the surprising comment of one of them. If Junior Savoyard No. 1 was referring to John Reed when he made his comment, I quite agree. Mr. Reed has a bad case of mime, as if he were used to playing largely to foreign audiences. I feel that a Ko-Ko has enough to do making the Gilbertian jokes funny by making them clear without setting up a side-circus. And to crown it all, Mr. Reed, who thinks that it is amusing to bring Gilbert and Sullivan up to date by introducing a Charleston, even stoops so low as to answer the Mikado's question about Nanki-Poo's whereabouts with, would you believe, "Forest Hill"?

Kenneth Sandfords's Pooh-Bah was blandness itself, of course, but there was a suggestion that the big balloon was not in full buoyancy last night.

If ever a reviewer illustrated the point that critiques are based on personal like or dislike, then Mr Whittaker did. Another critic to take a sharp swipe at John Reed was the *Toronto Globe and Mail*'s Blaik Kirby, in a review of *Iolanthe* at the O'Keefe Centre in May of 1978.

And what can be said of John Reed, the comedian who sang the Lord Chancellor? He has the experience to make a comic effect very well, but he sings like two sheets of sandpaper and can't keep in tempo.

In the same season, Kirby continued to snipe at John Reed, this time in *The Mikado*.

John Reed, the company's main comedian, was once again emphatic and lacking finesse in his comedy, and for the most part rough in his singing.

Others fared little better at the hands of Blaik Kirby.

Geoffrey Shovelton and Julia Goss, as the young lovers, showed good voices (and this company certainly needs them) but not really good performances. Kenneth Sandford was Pooh-Bah. He has always been Pooh-Bah, for more than 2,000 not-good-enough performances. His voice is not big enough, nor is his paunch.

It is easy to imagine that such cutting remarks might easily undermine principal performers. Without confidence and self-belief, going before an audience is almost impossible. Bad reviews may be an occupational hazard, but when they are couched in unnecessarily hostile language, they are very hurtful. The old saying 'It is not what you say, but the way that you say it' was never more appropriate. For D'Oyly Carters having to go on for the next show with such stinging comments echoing around their heads would have added enormously to the pressure felt before every live performance. Ignoring such personal attacks is never easy for a professional performer, but fighting back is not an option. Anger, distress and indignation have to be put aside in favour of hoping the next audience will make fairer judgement. For the D'Oyly Carte management, severe criticism of the company's in-house style and its failure to modernise the productions it staged was defended by unshakeable belief in its guardianship of Gilbert and Sullivan's original style.

For all the examples of severe criticism of the D'Oyly Carte and its performers, there were far more favourable 'crits' than bad during the course of lengthy North American tours. Some of those featured here contain examples of the sort of careless journalism which so infuriated performers. There are also reviews which lavish praise on the company and its artistes, some of them diametrically opposed to the sour comments from critics who pilloried the production and its individual performers during the same tour. Such was life at the hands of the press.

THE SAN FRANCISCO EXAMINER, SEPTEMBER 3RD, 1962

I have always had a fondness for "The Gondoliers" – that delightfully insane and melodic charade about royalty, which is perhaps the most polished and cutting of all the Gilbert and Sullivan satires. It was presented at the Geary over the weekend by the D'Oyly Carte Opera Company and I cannot remember when I have enjoyed it more. Though the mood of "The Gondoliers" is mock 18th century Venetian and Spanish (with a story that's utter madness), the humour is strictly Victorian English and George R. Foa's direction made the most of all the foolishness but with gem-like British restraint.

Thomas Round and Alan Styler were admirable as the two republican-minded gondoliers who were abruptly raised to the dual rank of king. And Jean Hindmarsh and Peggy Ann Jones made them deliciously bouncy Venetian wives. But the piece-de-resistance was offered by Kenneth Sandford, a baritone whose exquisite sense of humour had the sting of a serpent's tooth in the role of a Grand

Inquisitor who equips his torture chamber with illustrated daily papers.

The Boston Record, 1968

The D'Oyly Carte Opera Company is back in Boston and better than ever. At the Savoy Theater on Washington St., the Savoyards of London gave a perfect performance of Gilbert and Sullivan's "Patience" Tuesday evening. The word is perfect. Yes, there were occasional faults and lapses. Yes, some of the singers were occasionally less lucid in the elaborate lyrics than others. But the faults were tiny, minor, miniscule, the production was brilliantly sung, beautifully played in the high dry mock-comic style performers have always possessed and which is so exhilarating to watch. Call it perfect.

The San Francisco Examiner, May 1978

The older one gets, the less one feels like Queen Victoria. Sitting through D'Oyly Carte's Tuesday opening of "The Mikado", I was definitely amused. Julia Goss was a wonderfully scatter-brained Yum-Yum, scoring a real flight of song with her first entrance, "Three Little Girls in School". She, Jane Metcalfe and Roberta Moreel managed to clown while remembering their ladylike poses. Even the occasional Cockney "slips" were achieved with grace.

That the critic, Hewell Tircuit, should get the title of such a famous song so badly-wrong, not to mention the interesting spelling of my surname, did not encourage confidence in the capability of a journalist whose knowledge of his subject was so lacking and attention to the cast list so sloppy.

In the *Denver Post* of July 8th, 1968, Arlynn Nellhaus' review was headlined: *Yeoman is finely wrought.* Commenting on a performance at the Central City Opera House, this reviewer went on to say: *Fine voices and incisive characterisations marked the D'Oyly Carte of London's finely wrought Yeomen of the Guard. First there's Phoebe, who helped Fairfax escape because of her love for him. Peggy Ann Jones in the role is fresh-faced, saucy and mellow-voiced. You wish better than what she gets – Wilfred. She's* resigned, almost, to marrying the leaden, morose jailor and assistant tormentor. Kenneth Sanford's Wilfred is a man who comes to life with enthusiasm only when he considers the torture chamber or marriage to Phoebe.

No, that is not my typing mistake: Nellhaus' review had both *Yeoman* and *Yeomen* within a few lines and Sandford misspelled.

In the *Washington Post* of July 2nd, 1976, Richard L. Coe's review demonstrates that what one critic hates, another loves.

> *John Reed, the D'Oyly Carte's veteran, last night delighted two full houses at performances of H.M.S. Pinafore. That most nimble-tongued of Savoyards has a way with such words as monarch, ruler, anchor, here, ride, pride and breezes that make it possible for his Sir Joseph Porter, K.C.B., to stand still and keep every eye in the house riveted on what is, all others considered, a fairly small mouth. Reed is now in parts once thought to be eternally identified with George Grossmith, Henry Lytton and Martin Green. Now that it is Reed's turn in these roles that have a century of history, he is worthy of everything that's been said of his predecessors.*
>
> *Making his first appearance as Ralph Rackstraw, Meston Reid proves an outstanding tenor, tall, slim and boyish – and a fine new lead for the company. His Josephine, Barbara Lilley, is also most welcome. Michael Rayner sings well as Josephine's father, Capt. Corcoran.*

The earlier review of *Pinafore* by Kirby and this one by Coe, so far apart in their perception of the same production, lead one to wonder why they see things so differently. So which of them is right? The only conclusion to be drawn is that 'one man's meat is another man's poison'. Every review boils down to personal taste, but this fact is seldom made clear to the reader deciding on whether or not to attend a show.

The *New York Times* critic, Raymond Ericson, writing on May 6th, 1976 probably tips the balance away from Blaik Kirby.

> *It was the company's veterans, however, who gave this "Mikado" its special quality. Kenneth Sandford, who is credited with almost 2,000 performances as Pooh-Bah, still rolls out his lines and lyrics with the proper relish of Gilbert's wit. Then there was John Reed, making his sixth tour of North America in 20 years. He pranced through his part*

of Ko-Ko as if he hadn't aged a year. His comic spirit remains fresh,
and he sings the "Tit willow" song with a proper seductiveness that
is both sly and sad.

In the *Chicago Tribune* of May 17th, 1978, theatre critic, John Von
Rhein, praised the D'Oyly Carte for both its work and coping with the
amplification intended to improve the acoustics in the cavernous Arie
Crown Theater.

The Arie Crown's new sound system, which was receiving its official
baptism, carried the D'Oyly Carte voices effectively enough to my
front-section orchestra seat, though the theater's still-untamed
acoustics often turned the orchestra into an echoey, muffled hash.
But to compensate for the unfamiliar amplification, the singers and
conductor had evidently been instructed to enunciate every syllable
S-L-O-W-L-Y. This did not exactly further comic momentum or
enhance the built-in spirit of airy persiflage.

Still there were compensations. The measured pacing gave all
Titipuans a chance to savor those merry madrigals and titwillow
elegies with loving solicitude. And it afforded those wonderful old
Savoy hams, John Reed (Ko-Ko) and Kenneth Sandford (Pooh-Bah),
lots of time to milk a few extra laughs out of their well-routined but still
delightful bits of stage business. (Keep your eye on Sandford's rubber
tummy.) In short, like the merciful Mikado's after-lunch punishment
for Ko-Ko and cohorts, this "Mikado" was humorous – but lingering.

By now, Reed's fluttery body-British and naughty asides have
become as much a part of the venerable D'Oyly Carte tradition as
his encores. After 26 seasons with the company, he can still plunder
his patter songs for maximum mischief. Sandford intoned Pooh-
Bah's haughty platitudes with exquisite deliberation, as usual. If
there is any withering nuance this masterful comic actor hasn't yet
given us in the Lord High Everything Else, it simply does not exist.
Julia Goss, as Yum-Yum, and Geoffrey Shovelton, as Nanki-Poo,
made an attractive and vocally pleasing pair of lovers in the best,
insipidly sweet G&S tradition. The easily sonorous Shovelton was
a vast improvement over the adenoidal tenors the D'Oyly Carte has
inflicted on us in the past.

Royston Nash, the company's stylish music director, enforced reasonable elegance and warmth from the fine orchestra, though the generally stolid tempos dictated by acoustical circumstances got to be a bit of a bore before long. The unobtrusive setting, also a considerable improvement over the tacky flats seen here in the past, consisted of a neat Japanesy teahouse, pagoda and bridge framed by screens and flanked by picture-postcard drops. The costumes were similarly charming.

This detailed critique, presented by a man who thoroughly knew the show, the company and its artistes, surely did what it was meant to do in presenting a fair and honest assessment of what anyone thinking of attending could expect to see. This cleverly-crafted review is informative, witty and engaging. Not for him the biting criticism that characterised many a North American reviewer, just an honest opinion of what he saw and heard. Mr. Von Rhein was a rare animal indeed.

That reviewers could see and experience the same production, with the same cast, so differently, amply demonstrates the subjective nature of theatre criticism and the D'Oyly Carte principals came to expect this. Whichever of them took a hammering from a critic, the others were there to help them laugh off the harsh comments, with a reminder of all the good reviews. Such mutual support was typical, but stinging criticism is not that easy to forget. At 92 years of age, Cynthia Morey can still remember the caustic remarks of, perhaps, the most infamous American critic of all, the *Chicago Tribune*'s Claudia 'Acidy' Cassidy. Well-known in Chicago theatre circles for her decimation of many a famous artiste, on the 1956 D'Oyly Carte tour, she described Cynthia as *'skim milk masquerading as cream'*. Although showing a knowledge of G&S text, she used it without any care for the effect of her spiteful wit on her victim's feelings. Cynthia can now laugh about it, but to remember that review some sixty years later suggests feeling just a little humiliation at the time. And who could blame her? But the principals had been told about Claudia Cassidy, as Cynthia explains.

'We'd been warned well in advance about the sort of things she would say. I remember crowding round the newspaper the morning after with the others to read what she'd written – it was a sort of competition to see who got the worst notice. We regarded that as an accolade – of a kind!'

An artiste receiving a good account of their performance always wants to believe it, however unqualified the reviewer, their fragile ego boosted by complimentary words. However, anyone on the end of a slating from a theatre critic is often left embarrassed and upset, their confidence dented by harsh comments about their work. Having to get straight back on the horse after a bad review is no easy thing, but D'Oyly Carters regularly had to face this possibility, often on a weekly basis when on tour. An obvious solution was not to read them, but this was not always easy, especially if the Company Manager had put up the review on the theatre notice board, when the urge to find out what had been said was difficult to resist. Seasoned principals tended to shrug their shoulders and not worry, an approach recommended to their less-experienced colleagues on the basis of 'Some you win, some you lose', but that was easier said than done. Everyone likes to be praised, but no-one likes to be criticised.

Over many decades, D'Oyly Carte principals came to expect the mixed fortunes associated with North America's theatre critics. But, in 1979, the unique tour of Australia and New Zealand was an unknown quantity as far as reviews were concerned: the principals had no idea what to expect. It is right to say that there were some interesting critiques of the performances given by a Gilbert and Sullivan company from the other side of the world. Indeed, one reviewer seemed determined to find faults with the renowned British troupe, implying arrogance towards the audience which was a figment of journalistic imagination. Hard to believe maybe, but the reviewer with a nationalistic chip on his shoulder seemed convinced that D'Oyly Carte performers were not interested in Australian audiences. I was unable to find a name associated with the following review in the *Melbourne Sunday Observer* of July 29th, 1979, which is a pity; it would have been nice to name and shame the perpetrator.

Perhaps I went to the Princess Theatre last week expecting too much! The D'Oyly Carte Opera Company's presentation of "The Mikado" was in many ways disappointing. When a company is promoted as the best you expect to see the best. The Melbourne audience did not get a 100 per cent performance from the D'Oyly Carte company at the opening night of The Mikado. It appeared as though most of the performers in the production did not think much of the audience. Consequently they did not seem to give of their all.

I may be wrong, but it wouldn't be the first time an international group of performers has treated an Australian audience with less than respect. The audience seemed to laugh at anything and the performers appeared to react by giving them anything. Several Australianisms were sprinkled throughout the performance which in some cases were funny. Apart from the disappointments the night was not a complete waste. A few performances stood out including John Reed as Ko-Ko, the Lord High Executioner, who together with a good voice was able to capture the character. I suppose he should have, he has been with the company for 25 years. Melbourne didn't see the best performance of the sorry wandering minstrel, Nanki-Poo, falling in love with Yum-Yum, the executioner's wife, but it was reasonable.

Such arrant nonsense was nothing short of insulting to a company of dedicated, professional performers. The idea that everyone on stage collectively thought the Australian audience unworthy of their best efforts is, plainly, silly. But perhaps there is a clue to the credibility of this paranoid, second-rate hack in the final line of the review. If he or she knew G&S well enough to qualify them to make criticism, they would have been aware that 'Yum-Yum' is not the bride of the executioner, 'Ko-Ko', but merely his betrothed. I rest my case.

Another opinionated scribbler who couldn't wait to get his knife into the D'Oyly Carte and explain where the company had gone wrong penned this review for the *Melbourne Herald* of July 24th, 1979. Again, despite research, I can find no name attached to it.

For the hundreds of ardent Savoyards who gathered at the shrine last night the D'Oyly Carte Company remained the true defender of the faith. To them, the company, in its long-awaited Melbourne debut, could do no wrong and every number, every joke was tumultuously applauded. Giving comic theatre last night they were superb. But giving an opera, even a light one, they were not.

The stars, so brilliant visually, exaggerated their roles as they wrung the most from every moment so that they continually upstaged each other, and worse, the music. Musical opinion generally holds that Sullivan sacrificed his gifts to those of Gilbert. In turning "The Mikado" into high farce, the D'Oyly Carte almost did away with them. An example. In the trio "Here's a how-de-do" Ko-Ko unfurls an Australian flag, which is funny. But the number becomes merely a vehicle for Ko-Ko as he stretches it interminably with fans, flowers, knitting, a trolley ride across the stage etc., repeating the trio each time. Gilbert's wit stands best alone: such extremes become intrusive.

That major reservation aside, the performance could barely be faulted. John Reed made Ko-Ko, the Lord High Executioner, a beautifully abject buffoon, engaging and hilarious, while Kenneth Sandford was a magnificently pompous Pooh-Bah, the Lord High Everything Else who is one of the comic theatre's immortal creations.

Given this reviewer's serious accusation that star performers lacked stage craft and 'continually upstaged each other', overdid comedy business and did no service to Gilbert's wit, the contradictory nature of the critique is little short of ridiculous. It is likely that this person had no idea as to the true meaning of 'upstaging', but D'Oyly Carte principals most certainly did and never committed such a basic mistake. It is a classic example of personal opinion, more about the ego of the journalist anxious to air his knowledge and patronise the audience than serving the public interest.

At least there was one happy Australian bunny, W.L. Hormann, who wrote this review in the Canberra press on May 16th, 1979:

Tradition can be a dull and deadening thing; but the English have been able to maintain so many of theirs as 'living traditions', and the D'Oyly Carte Opera Company demonstrates very vividly that this can apply to musical traditions such as G&S as well.

On Monday night it opened its first Australian tour at the Canberra Theatre with a delightful production of 'Iolanthe', a production so different from what we usually see as G&S that some people may feel a little disappointed on seeing it. 'Iolanthe' is one of the more 'serious' Savoy Operas but if it is played too seriously it becomes dull, and if, as is more usually the case, it is played too lightly it becomes mere farce.

To me, this production gets closer to the real intent of the words and the music than any other I have seen: but those who like their

G&S 'hammed up' may think otherwise. The humour is there, but delightfully understated as in the playing of John Ayldon (Earl of Mountararat) and Meston Reid (Earl Tolloller), and in a most engaging performance by Kenneth Sandford as Private Willis. And the ladies are not outdone, with an imposing yet quietly humorous Queen of the Fairies from Patricia Leonard, an Iolanthe in Lorraine Daniels who certainly looked too young to be Strephon's mother, and excellent singing support from the rest of the fairies.

This refreshingly thoughtful assessment is a rare example of a critic who makes it clear why he likes what he has seen, with the honesty to recognise that others may not agree with him. It is also one of the few examples of principals, other than the company's 'big names' getting a mention. How frustrating it must have been for the other leading performers, who worked tirelessly at a high professional level, to so seldom be deemed worthy of being named. It might be supposed that no comment was better than critical comment, but a good 'crit' was always something for the scrapbook.

Having explored the nature of reviews of D'Oyly Carte performances from North America and Australia, what of the British press? By far the majority of critiques of the company came from home journalists who, like their overseas counterparts, varied in quality and style. In general, provincial newspaper reviews tended to be shorter and less-detailed than those appearing in the London press. Annual London seasons were always covered by such newspapers as *The Times, The Guardian* and *The Telegraph*, whose music and theatre journalists were well-known for their in-depth knowledge of the subjects they covered. For a D'Oyly Carte principal, a good review in the top London press was deemed important for their career and always eagerly-awaited with a mixture of hope and trepidation. A performance heavily criticised was, inevitably, devastating. Sometimes, reviews appeared in the *London Evening Standard*, the *Daily Express* and the *Daily Mail*, when good ink was always welcome, but never as much as when delivered by the heavyweight newspapers.

Away from the capital, reviews in papers such as the *Yorkshire Post*, the *Manchester Evening News* or the *Birmingham Post* were considered important, but the local press of most towns too often lacked journalists qualified to give informed coverage. From the management point of view, as long as a newspaper report was positive enough to encourage audience attendance, it was content and the occasional bad review was considered to make little difference, because support for the D'Oyly Carte was always strong.

The following extracts and reviews from both the London press and provincial newspapers illustrate how very different they were in approach, style and content.

In *The Times* of April 7th, 1971, the well-respected critic, Alan Blyth, reviewed the D'Oyly Carte's revival of *The Sorcerer* at the Manchester Opera House.

Gilbert and Sullivan celebrate their centenary together next December, although 'Thespis', performed in 1871, is lost. The pair's next collaboration was on 'Trial by Jury', but it was 'The Sorcerer', in 1877 that first brought them and D'Oyly Carte together on a more-or-less permanent basis. It ran for 178 performances, good enough by any standard other than that of its even more popular successors. The work was revised and given some new numbers for the 1884 revival, but by then the three Ps, 'Patience', 'Pinafore' and 'Pirates' were putting 'The Sorcerer' in the shade.

The production that opened in Manchester last Monday is in fact the first since 1939 – the previous production was lost in the war – and this neglect seems uncalled for. The plot, based on the idea of the administration of a love potion in an early version of the "make love not war" formula, is admittedly thin, but all the well-known fingerprints of the G&S partnership are already visible. On Gilbert's side we have elderly, ugly women (two of them here!), lovelorn young ladies, an aimless aristocratic young man, a silly-billy cleric and a droll sorcerer. Sullivan provides pretty, none-too-exacting music (for singers) and neat orchestration, with finely-turned ensembles. His music is cosmopolitan in the sense that it followed the Mendelssohn-Weber tradition – the Incantation is a feeble, genteel version of 'The Wolf's Glen' (surely not a parody of it); insular, in the sense that by the 1870s that sort of bland, mellifluous tune-spinning had had its day on the Continent. 'The Sorcerer' was only the beginning of a series that exploits a tired idiom.

Michael Heyland's bright, stylish but rather too traditional production will please the faithful. So will Osbert Lancaster's slightly irreverent sets, which call to mind his Glyndebourne programme-book covers, even the house and garden themselves, down to an outsize clematis. Sometimes the dialogue went too slowly, and surely Aline, having taken her philtre, should become gradually infatuated with the Rev. Dr. Daly during his melancholy "Oh, my voice is sad and low". The part of this bumbling but jaunty vicar was in the safe hands and voice of Kenneth Sandford. His true love, Constance, brought forward Linda Anne Hutchison, one of the company's brighter hopes. The part, surely a soprano's, lay rather high for her pleasing mezzo. John Reed, of course, took the Sorcerer himself, John Wellington Wells, who has the show's single well-known number, which was despatched with Reed's usual brio. Elsewhere, he was inclined to forget his assumed cockney accent and fall back into G&S 'refained' English.

Royston Nash, who has just taken over as the company's conductor, kept things moving and already has the authentic Sullivan lilt at his command. The playing, too, was much improved.

On the 6ᵗʰ of June, 1981, this review appeared in the *Eastern Daily Press*.

Why Gilbert and Sullivan's 'The Sorcerer' is not performed more often, by amateur companies as well as the pros, has always puzzled me – it's so full of good fun, good tunes and character roles. That the D'Oyly Carte Opera Company who present it so sparklingly, as they illustrated last night at the Theatre Royal Norwich, should now withdraw it altogether from their repertoire, is quite incomprehensible.

When the company opened their two-week stay in Norwich last Monday, it was a pleasure to note the new vitality which had entered into them since they were publicly pilloried by the Arts Council. With just a few minor reservations, this splendidly enjoyable 'Sorcerer' more than maintains that impression.

The D'Oyly Carte are now fighting for their existence. On the strength of this last two weeks, they deserve to win. But were I to be devil's advocate for the Arts Council – which the gods forbid – I'd suggest that the exhilarating spring cleaning they've evidenced during this fortnight, though well advanced, is not yet wholly completed. May they finish the job – and live for many a year to come.

The Times' legendary theatre critic, Stanley Sadie, wrote this review on January 9th, 1981.

The D'Oyly Carte company, as usual at this time of the year, are on show in London, just at the moment of the body blow administered to them by the Arts Council. Devotees of the Savoy operettas have long had mixed feelings about the company that stands as their custodian: that on the one hand it guards an unbroken tradition, that on the other it has lived too long and too easily on that tradition and has taken too little trouble to protect it other than by keeping it jellied in increasingly cloudy aspic.

Whether the Arts Council's withdrawal need mean the death of the company, and whether the death of the company need mean the extinction of the tradition, are of course further questions. The company itself, on the evidence of last night's 'Yeomen of the Guard' – which is far from the most vivacious piece in their repertory – is understandably sounding dispirited.

It needs first of all to regain something of its musical professionalism. There was more uncertain intonation and ensemble in this revival than anyone could reasonably justify, most of it, I thought, arising from an unwanted inflexibility in Fraser Goulding's direction. For a company that subsists on Gilbert and Sullivan operas, it ought not be necessary for liaison between singer and orchestra to falter every time there is a "patter song". In much of Jack Point's rapid music, and not only there, things came unhinged; it should be possible to work out in advance where breaths are needed, where words need more time to be clearly articulated, and where they need to be pressed forward. And almost everything would have profited from more sparkle and spirit.

Some of the stage business, too, though by no means all of it, looks to be loosely executed. For singers, the D'Oyly Carte has long served as a nursery. There are no Valerie Mastersons around at the moment, it seems, but there were some neat and pointed impersonations. Lorraine

Daniels, the Phoebe, sang and acted with a charming coquetry after an unsure vocal start. Barbara Lilley's Elsie was tasteful, but the vibrato seems almost out of control. Patricia Leonard's Dame Carruthers is firmly in the old tradition, if less juicy than some.

Best of the men were Geoffrey Shovelton, a tenor who phrases Fairfax's lines cleanly and musically and Kenneth Sandford, whose Wilfred has many good things (including a good firm baritone) if not the full moroseness. James Conroy-Ward brings a hint of elegance to his quite touching portrayal of Jack Point. But I wonder if the exaggerated drama school diction that he and most of the cast bring to their lines is really an essential part of the tradition. I hope D'Oyly Carte will manage some stiff self-criticism, including a hard look at what those traditions really mean, and will reform themselves to a point where all British industry is eager to pay to keep them on the boards.

A review by the well-respected Arthur Jacobs which appeared in the *Musical Times* in 1970 again demonstrates that a knowledgeable and opinionated theatre critic left no place to hide for anyone associated with a D'Oyly Carte production.

To open the D'Oyly Carte season at Sadler's Wells on December 15th, Princess Ida was exhumed rather than revived. The old, unconvincing scenery by James Wade, badly lit (the 1964 staging at least had Michael Northern to light it), the tired-out dance steps and gestures, the routined encores, one of them quite unprovoked – such presentation will not suffice to validate this piece, crippled from birth by an outdated satire and a plot which lacks proper climax. On the credit side, the engagement of the Philomusica gave some chance to Sullivan's orchestrations, though by the second night James Walker had not always scaled down the instrumental sound enough to let the modest voices through.

Mr. Walker, who served an apprenticeship under Isidore Godfrey and has now succeeded him as the company's musical director, gives no sign of a new broom. The continued omission of Lady Blanche's aria – however traditional the omission, however weak the aria – simply upsets the total balance and makes total nonsense of Lady Blanche's later allusion to the words of that aria. The chorus needs strengthening, preferably in number as well as quality, and a new Hildebrand should replace the veteran Kenneth Sandford. Ida herself, the only approximation in G&S to the category of dramatic soprano, demands a more powerful voice than Valerie Masterson exhibited – handicapped, admittedly, by having to sing 'O goddess wise' from the back of the stage.

Sullivan's style here has many felicities, few weak patches, and several harmonic ingenuities which (particularly in the finale of the second act) still surprise and please. But the score seems not quite to catch the three-act dramatic span. Gama's two songs, stylishly but too predictably delivered by John Reed, are too similar, and the comedy hardly takes wing in the music until the three young male invaders of the women's college have assumed women's disguise. All these three (Philip Potter, Ralph Mason, Thomas Lawlor) were admirable – though a high B flat instead of A at the end of the kissing song spoils the piquancy of Sullivan's 9th-chord. Of the girls, Melissa (Pauline Wales) was a charmer.

A review of *Princess Ida* in the *Eastern Daily Press* during the company's 1977 season in Norwich could not provide a greater contrast. Short and sweet, it neatly sums up the difference between the serious London newspapers and those in the provinces. Headlined *'Daft yet adorable, that's Ida'*, its low-tech approach provides only one serious instance of actual criticism.

In Ida's never-never land, she's created a ladies' university where the male in all his forms is rigorously excluded (even cock-crowing is celebrated by a singularly accomplished hen). But Ida (Barbara Lilley) was espoused at one year of age, in one of those quixotic Gilbertian turns of plot which turn up more than once in the G&S repertoire, to Hilarion, son of bellicose King Hildebrand, who 20 years later is determined to enforce the match.

Now there's a daft and adorable plot for you. But you forgive it when it provides such opportunities for Kenneth Sandford, as Hildebrand, and John Reed, as the heroine's disagreeable old pa, King Gama.

Sandford has spent so long playing in grandiose costumes that he does it to the life (catch a glimpse of his stately stride off-duty and

41

you'll see what I mean!) And with this particular costume – mythical Atlantis visualised by the designer of "Up Pompeii" – he cannot and does not fail. Great stuff, great comedy. Though the repeatedly low-pitching of some of the king's songs does give his high baritone some minor difficulties, damping down the vocal clarity and projection of which he is normally a master.

Given that *Princess Ida* boasts a large cast, such a critique must surely have made the other principals despair, their names and contribution ignored in what cannot be taken seriously as a theatre review. Whether or not it encouraged audience attendance is open to debate, but to concentrate almost exclusively on one performer in such a short piece seems decidedly odd. That 'star' D'Oyly Carte performers took most of the plaudits was par for the course, as the following brief, meaningless report in the *Western Mail* of July 30th, 1957 clearly demonstrates.

The Tower of London is rather old. The story of a romantic prisoner and the lovesick maid who engineers his release is also rather smitten with age. But mix the two together, add a background of brilliantly-clad yeomen giving voice to stirring melodies, and you have that mixture of sentiment and ceremonial against which few Britons are proof.

Peter Pratt (as Jack Point, the strolling jester) was light of foot and successfully garrulous in a part which called for an equal measure of prancing and garrulity. One of his main foils was lumbering Wilfred Shadbolt, head gaoler and assistant tormentor, played by Kenneth Sandford. This swarthy denizen of the Tower sang the foolish words of a foolish suitor, but how good they sounded in his fine baritone.

Two days later, an even shorter, not to mention inaccurate, review appeared in the *South Wales Echo*, but at least it featured five names.

Like an apple tree, Gilbert and Sullivan's "The Gondoliers" flourishes and blossoms. It starts slowly, almost too slowly, but the second half is a riot. I thought that the D'Oyly Carte production at the New Theatre, Cardiff, last night rather reflected that.

But for me, the highlight was that magnificent quartet "In A Contemplative Mood" sung with great spirit by Neville Griffiths

(Marco), Alan Styler (Giuseppe), Joyce Wright (Tessa) and the fine voiced Jean Hindmarsh (Gianetta). A word, too, for the Grand Inquisitor, sung beautifully by Kenneth Sandford.

Finally, from that same Cardiff season, another offering which leaves much to be desired, although it does, for once, feature the chorus.

Japan has invaded Cardiff – but only on the stage of the New Theatre, Cardiff. The D'Oyly Carte Opera Company are here again and open a fortnight of Gilbertian spectacles with the ever popular "Mikado". As far as the solo parts are concerned it may be that "When A is happy B is not "since many hold strong views on how Gilbert and Sullivan should be sung, but the chorus work would undoubtedly have gained even the approval of one of those early critical Edwardian audiences.

The story of the Town of Titipu, where flirting is capital, needs no introduction, though several of the singers do. Maureen Melvin makes a charming Yum-Yum, tripping about and singing brightly with a roguish lilt in the eye which is lost occasionally in a downward demure cast. Also the company's new Pooh-Bah, Kenneth Sandford. He looks a tremendous swell in his Lord-High-Everything-Else's yellow robes.

These are but a few examples of the work of the theatre critic and it must be said that, in this time-scale covering four decades of reviews, there will have been instances of provincial journalists whose knowledge of Gilbert and Sullivan was exemplary, but they were a rarity. However, one thing is certain, D'Oyly Carte performers felt pressure when it came to being reviewed on a regular basis. It was not easy having to contend with both good and bad ink, sometimes heavily criticised and sometimes feted, when they never knew which it was going to be. Although being scrutinised came with the job, bad reviews and home truths always hurt and embarrassed, particularly when coming from an eminent theatre critic, but a good review was welcome from any quarter. It is probably safe to say that the Carters scrapbooks were full of good reviews: why would they keep the bad ones?

CHAPTER THREE

ON THE ONE HAND ...

The enormous and enduring popularity of the comic operas of Gilbert and Sullivan is little short of astonishing. That the D'Oyly Carte Opera Company successfully presented them for over a century is no less astonishing and a tribute to its sound business operation in attracting huge audiences right to the end of its long life, when the escalating cost of touring without public funding finally led to its demise in 1982. From its inception, the company boasted a huge following, due to the glorious music and hilarious satire of the thirteen Savoy Operas and the generations of talented singers who performed them. The D'Oyly Carte seasons in towns and cities across the country were eagerly anticipated by young and old alike, the appearance of the famous company and its stars a source of great pleasure which, for many, lasted throughout their lifetime. At times of change, the D'Oyly Carte was unchanging and devoted followers flocked to theatres, many booking to see every show in the repertoire. Before and after every performance, the Stage Door was besieged by devoted fans brandishing autograph books, photographs and programmes to be signed by their heroes, regardless of how many times they had previously gained these prized signatures.

But it was not just in Great Britain that the D'Oyly Carte was enormously popular. In America and Canada, audiences welcomed the regular visits by the famous Gilbert and Sullivan company which had travelled across the Atlantic from its earliest days in the 1870s. G&S was as popular there as it was in its homeland, the delights of *The Mikado*, *The Pirates of Penzance* and *HMS Pinafore*, in particular, being perennial favourites across the pond. Similar throngs of adoring fans patiently waited outside American theatres to catch a glimpse of the stars so adept in the art of presenting Gilbert and Sullivan. For the many devotees of G&S in Australia and New Zealand, the one-off tour Down Under in 1979 was the only opportunity to see the historic D'Oyly Carte Opera Company, made famous to them by the company's recordings of the Savoy Operas. To this day, wherever in the world English speakers live and work, an amateur performing group is never too far away, bringing the popular operettas not only to North America, but also to such countries as South Africa, Belgium, Switzerland and Malta.

So what kind of people were these fans? Was there something which characterised the type of person who slavishly followed the D'Oyly Carte Opera Company? The simple answer is no. From the company's earliest times, fans could be identified from all classes of society. The raucous renditions of popular G&S tunes in the Victorian taverns of London, or the rather more sedate humming of the same melodies in Buckingham Palace would indicate their infectious charm across the social spectrum. They were the pop songs of their time. It has been well-documented that Queen Victoria hosted D'Oyly Carte performances at Windsor Castle and Balmoral, whilst our present monarch, Queen Elizabeth II, commanded a performance of *HMS Pinafore* at Windsor as part of her Silver Jubilee celebrations in 1977, which she considered to be a private party for family and friends.

Today, some thirty-eight years after the company closed down, social media plays its part in banding together lovers of Gilbert and Sullivan around the world on Facebook and Savoynet, whilst many British universities boast their own Gilbert and Sullivan societies, happily introducing another generation to the delights of G&S. It is to be hoped that these young people will go on to join amateur operatic societies and perpetuate interest in the Savoy Operas. With the annual International Gilbert and Sullivan Festival attracting thousands of people each year and many opera companies including G&S in their repertoires, there is a bright future to back up the good work of the hundreds of amateur Gilbert and Sullivan groups around the world. But, as the years go by, fewer and fewer people will remember, or know, anything about the D'Oyly Carte Opera Company, so it is important to document the people whose devotion kept it going for over a hundred years. There were certainly some colourful characters amongst them!

David Edwards can be considered a devoted D'Oyly Carte fan. His life-long love affair with the company began in the mid-1960s, when he appeared in Gilbert and Sullivan productions at secondary school. Once bitten by the G&S bug, he wanted to see as many of the operas as possible and that was when he first encountered the D'Oyly Carte Opera Company. At his local theatre in Wimbledon, the company was booked for a four-week run, during which most of the operas were to be performed, so he was in for an entertaining month. The seats in the gallery cost the princely sum of two shillings and sixpence (the equivalent of 12p today). Seating was on padded boards with no backrest, but once the show had started, all discomfort was forgotten. By the end of the season, he was hooked and read in the programme that there existed an organisation called 'The Friends of D'Oyly Carte', which he immediately joined. Membership gave him details of the company's touring schedule and a copy of *The Savoyard*, the in-house magazine with all the company news both on and off the stage, the arrival of which was always eagerly anticipated. Also at this time, he began collecting the company's recordings, treasured possessions which he still has to this day. His bedroom wall bore a map of the UK, helping him to plot the dates on the D'Oyly Carte's tours, his excitement mounting whenever they were playing in London and the South East. Before seeing a show, he would go early to the Stage Door and wait, his trusty camera capturing his favourite performers arriving at the theatre.

In his early days as a fan waiting at the Stage Door, he had to rely on seasoned fans to point out which of the performers was which, because it was difficult to recognise the stars he so admired when they were out of make-up and in 'civvies'. That soon changed and he dreamed of joining the famous company to be like the idols with whom he enjoyed chatting after a performance. Although this was not to be, he continued as a keen fan and went on to become a Music Director for amateur groups in the South East, conducting most of the Savoy Operas.

One of David's happiest memories is a Stage Door encounter with Peggy Ann Jones, when he gave her a box of chocolates. Her response was to offer him a backstage tour the next time the company was playing locally. Convinced she would not remember, he was thrilled when she did, taking him onto the set of *The Mikado* after a performance at the Granada Theatre in Sutton, where he walked in the footsteps of his heroes. It was a day he will never forget. His passion for the company is summed up in his own words.

'I would like to say a great big thank you to the D'Oyly Carte and all the wonderful company members for the many years of sheer delight they gave both to me and the many other fans all over the world. I feel privileged to have been able to see the company perform many times in my life and very much regret that it had to close down in 1982.'

Peggy must have had a soft spot for young men she met outside the theatre. The internationally-renowned Canadian conservationist and author of numerous wildlife books, Ronald Orenstein, recalls her taking pity on him when he missed his bus home after chatting with her at the Stage Door in Oxford. He has always remembered her kindness and treasures the friendship that ensued. Ron's own recollections delightfully describe the impact the D'Oyly Carte has had on his life.

'I became a convinced Gilbert and Sullivan enthusiast in the early 1960s. From 1960 to 1963 I attended a summer arts camp near Parry Sound in Ontario, where we not only produced *Trial By Jury* and a cut-down *Mikado* (I played Pooh-Bah, my first G&S role), but trooped off to Stratford, Ontario, where we saw Tyrone Guthrie's unforgettable productions of *Pinafore* and *Pirates*. I was hooked. My introduction to the D'Oyly Carte, though, was less dramatic: the only way I knew to expand my G&S horizons was by listening to their recordings, borrowed from the Toronto music library or – if I was lucky – bought.

'By the time I saw the company in person, I had joined the Toronto branch of the Gilbert and Sullivan Society, read everything I could on Savoy lore, and begun to appear in a few community productions.

Naturally, I was a rapt audience member for every opera included on the company tour – magical experiences all, even in the cavernous depths of Toronto's O'Keefe Centre. Better still, as a member of the G&S Society, I got to meet the performers – heroes all in my eyes – in the flesh. The G&S Society took it upon itself to make sure the company members were properly entertained (though I confess, looking back on it now, that my enthusiastic attempts to meet as many of my idols as possible may not have come across as entertainment for them). Nonetheless, the people I met couldn't have been nicer. Donald Adams – surely the owner of one of the most voluminous laughs ever to issue from a human throat – was unforgettable. Anthony Raffell and Pauline Wales were particularly patient with me and, of course, this was my first meeting with Peggy Ann Jones.

'A few years later, now a high school graduate, I found myself in Oxford, annoying famous scientists at the 1966 International Ornithological Congress with the same enthusiasm I had unleashed on the D'Oyly Carte performers in Toronto. They included, by the way, the original James Bond, an authority on Caribbean birds, who had allowed Ian Fleming to make use of his name. By sheer serendipity, the D'Oyly Carte was not only appearing in Oxford at the time, but also performing *Ruddigore*, an opera they had neglected to bring to Canada. I kept a journal of the occasion, and I hope anyone who finds the style of the following a bit pompous will consider my tender years and forgive me.'

Oxford, July 26th, 1966: The D'Oyly Carte is in town and I had a ticket for Ruddigore tonight. I tried to find some of my old acquaintances first, but located only Peggy Ann Jones, who did not remember me. She's the most friendly person alive, though. Ruddigore was brilliantly done. I know the gestures to a T, but to see them done with such flair and skill is breathtaking. The cast was excellent. Peggy Ann was a hilarious little Mad Margaret, scuttling about – not so much a lunatic as a harmless nut, very childlike. Kenneth Sandford was the best I have seen him as Despard and Ann Hood was radiant as Rose. Donald Adams was superb as usual, and John Reed was very good indeed – and so on. The new contralto, Christene Palmer, is a good Hannah but seems rather a small woman for the Fairy Queen or Katisha. The chorus of men was rather tired, but the girls were sprightly as can be. Lots of encores by the way. Afterwards I met Donald Adams and Pauline Wales, both of whom remembered me! I met Peggy again and she drove me back here, which was very kind – we had a wrong turning or so, but she isn't the type to faze easily. I may go back Friday for Iolanthe.

'To tell the truth, I was quite dumbstruck that a star of the D'Oyly Carte had actually offered me a lift home from the theatre. I never forgot it. Peggy Ann did not come on the company's next North American tour, during which I ended up conducting a radio interview with the Company Manager, Herbert Newby, who was, I think, a bit nonplussed on being asked why the company hadn't revived *Utopia Limited* or *The Grand Duke*. I didn't see her again for decades.

'The next time was courtesy of Ian Smith, at one of the first G&S festivals in Buxton. She didn't remember me, or her kindness to me at all, but she was as friendly as ever. Over the next few years we became friends. I was, at times, a guest at her home on my occasional visits to England. Once, she showed me the film of the animated *Ruddigore*, then an almost unobtainable rarity, with commentary by Mad Margaret herself – what a treat! She even whisked me off for a trip to Buxton, where some of the D'Oyly Carte veterans were giving a concert (and where I met John Reed for the first and only time). It's now been some years, alas, since I saw Peggy Ann, but she is not someone you can easily forget. I am grateful indeed for having had the opportunity to progress from a fan to a friend. So here's to you Peggy Ann, with much love and thanks for everything from "Big Ron", as you took to calling me – and I hope that we can meet again!'

Ronald Orenstein's experience of kindness towards D'Oyly Carte's fans from the company members was by no means unique. Alvin Entin was living in New Jersey when he became a fan of G&S through listening to the company's Decca recordings of the late 1940s and early '50s. From time to time, he persuaded his parents to take him to New York to see the American Savoyards, but he just knew that real G&S meant the D'Oyly Carte and he continued to collect its recordings. The first time he actually saw the company was while he was at college in Washington DC in the late 1960s, when it was appearing at the

49

National Theater. Arriving early at the Stage Door, he was approached by a grey-haired man who pleasantly asked what he was doing there.

'I suppose I gushed and tried to explain all the reasons I was there and why I was so obviously excited. I mentioned how much I missed the contralto star, Ann Drummond-Grant, on the recent recordings, two or three of which had been released in the mid-1960s without her in the "dame" roles. He seemed to be interested in what I had said and told me that she had been his wife, but that she had passed away. It was then that I found out that I was talking to Isidore Godfrey, the company's music director. He was as friendly and engaging as could be and invited me to come to the Stage Door after the show, when he would take me backstage to meet the cast and get autographs. I did, meeting John Reed and Donald Adams et al. It was a near perfect day which I have never forgotten.'

At the same time as Ron and Alvin were learning to love G&S from D'Oyly Carte recordings, on the other side of the world the distinguished New Zealand broadcaster, Des Wilson, had been doing much the same. At the age of twelve, he was given an album of 78 rpm recordings containing a complete performance of *The Mikado*, which he later discovered was the first official company recording, supervised by Richard D'Oyly Carte. It featured no performers from the company of the time, but used freelance singers instead. As other recordings followed, company members were gradually introduced so that, by the mid-1920s, most of the singers were current company members. This development sparked Des's fascination with recordings of Gilbert and Sullivan, so that when he started work and had money to spend, he set about buying all the D'Oyly Carte vinyl records then on the market. As the years went by, he obtained every complete G&S recording he could find, but his real interest was always with those made by D'Oyly Carte.

'For those of us living Down Under with no D'Oyly Carte tours coming our way, we had the next best thing. For many years, the Australian J.C. Williamson Company mounted extensive tours of Australia and New Zealand comprising several of the more popular operas, giving long seasons in the major cities. I am just old enough to have caught the last of these in 1957. Looking back, it seems incredible that the company spent a week in the small provincial city where I was then living, playing over the course of five consecutive nights the five full-length operas in the repertoire, plus two curtain raisers. For a long time, these tours had several ex-D'Oyly Carte singers appearing. I was able to see Graham Clifford, who had played the comedy roles while Martyn Green was absent during the war, Richard Walker, who sang the 'Mikado' roles, with his wife, Helen Roberts as principal soprano, the greatly-admired Richard Watson in the 'Pooh-Bah' parts and Eric Thornton, whose voice was familiar to me from his one appearance on record as Mountararat in *Iolanthe*. More recently, my researches have shown that amongst ex-Carters who were on these tours before my time were James Hay, Frederick Hobbs, Sydney Granville, Ivan Menzies, Gregory Stroud, Leo Darnton, Dorothy Gill, Evelyn Gardiner, Winifred Lawson, Lesley Rands and Marjorie Eyre. But the earliest of them all must surely have been Leonora Braham, the original Patience, Princess Ida, Yum-Yum and Rose Maybud, who appeared in Australia as early as 1888. I was told that these productions were traditional in that they were staged very much in the manner of the D'Oyly Carte, with no changes to the words and music.

'I never dreamed back in 1957 that the D'Oyly Carte Opera Company would ever come as far as Australia and New Zealand, so you can imagine the excitement when I learned that this was to happen in 1979. I was so pleased to see that the opera to be played in Wellington was to be *Iolanthe*, one of my favourites, but in the event, it didn't even get across the Tasman, so we had *Mikado* instead. I half-knew what to expect, I think, in that I had seen the film that had been made, so was familiar with the performances of John Reed and Kenneth Sandford. And from their records I knew the voices of John Ayldon and Philip Potter. I couldn't help thinking how tired the company must have felt after all the travelling, but there was not a hint of it in the performance. Being a traditionalist and hating to see my beloved operas mucked about, I loved every minute of it. I still remember, during one of the encores of "Here's a how-de-do", John Reed being hauled across the stage sitting on a little trolley, wearing hugely oversized spectacles and knitting on equally big needles. What fun!'

Another of the many G&S fans to be thrilled by the prospect of the D'Oyly Carte coming to Australia was Diana Burleigh. Having grown up in England, she had seen the company some two hundred times in various parts of the UK before emigrating. Having so much missed seeing the shows D'Oyly Carte-style, she was delighted by the prospect of enjoying its performances again. In 1979, she was living in Melbourne, where she had her own radio programme, but couldn't wait for them to arrive in her home town, so she took a trip to Canberra, the opening date of the tour. Relishing the D'Oyly Carte shows, she met many members of the company and found out from principal tenor, Meston Reid, that one of his hobbies was visiting the graves of famous people. He told her that he was anxious to see that of the great Australian singer, Nellie Melba, whereupon she told him that she would be happy to take him there and also try to arrange a visit to Melba's home. Using her contacts, she got in touch with Lady Viola Tait, widow of Sir Frank Tait, one of a group of brothers who had run the earlier-mentioned J.C. Williamson Company's Gilbert and Sullivan tours. Lady Viola had been a principal soprano with the D'Oyly Carte between 1938 and 1939, before accepting an offer to join the Williamson organisation.

Although herself unavailable, Lady Viola arranged for Diana to take a small group of Carters to have a private tour of Melba's home, before visiting her impressive grave. She recalls there being two cars of people, but cannot now remember all those who accompanied Meston Reid, except chorus members, Elizabeth Denham, Jillian Mascall and Paul Weakley. The fascinating tour of the house by the housekeepers revealed it to be much as Melba left it, right down to the dresses hung in her wardrobe. The pleasure of the visit for Meston, in particular, was matched by that of Diana, who was thrilled to be able to entertain members of her beloved D'Oyly Carte. She also mentions taking principal soprano, Vivian Tierney and her husband, baritone Gareth Jones, on a tour of the wineries in the Barossa Valley. The three-week season in Melbourne offered Diana ample opportunity to be involved with the company but, on hearing that John Reed was to leave the company at the end of the tour, she went to Sydney to get a final fix of the great 'patter man'. Her interest in G&S has continued long after the demise of the D'Oyly Carte in 1982 and she is still actively involved with directing productions of the Savoy Operas.

Back in the UK, in the early 1960s, a young man called Ken Foley had an amusing introduction to the delights of Gilbert and Sullivan. His good friend, Bill Jones, was already a devoted fan of the D'Oyly Carte and the Savoy operas as Ken relates.

'Bill would make constant references to the dialogue and lyrics, with the occasional burst into song. When Christmas came around, I decided to buy him a recording of *The Mikado* by, dare I say it, Sadler's Wells Opera Company. Before wrapping up the double record album, inquisitiveness got the better of me, so I thought I would play the first side and make my own judgement. My portable record player was for my Bill Haley and Elvis Presley recordings and the sound quality was not brilliant, but it would suffice for what I wanted. I picked out side one of the first record and began to play the overture which, I thought, wasn't at all bad – in fact, I rather liked it. However, when the gentlemen began with the opening chorus "If you want to know who we are", not only did they seem to be singing in falsetto, but also at an alarming speed. Yes, I was playing the LP at 45rpm instead of the necessary 33rpm! An inauspicious start, but it kicked off my lifelong love of Gilbert and Sullivan.'

Thereafter, Ken always attended D'Oyly Carte performances at the Alexandra Theatre in Birmingham and Wolverhampton's Grand Theatre along with friend Bill and two other friends, John and Jean Wood. During one Wolverhampton season, Ken recalls a very awkward moment, which haunts him to this day.

'I believe it was around 1965 and the four of us, as always after a performance, radiated to the Dress Circle bar. Occasionally, performers relaxing after the show could be seen taking well-earned refreshment and, on this particular occasion, we were delighted to see principal tenor, Ralph Mason, a particular favourite of John's. In no time at all we had engaged with the very genial Ralph and probably bored him to death with our incessant questions. After another show later in the week, we were in the bar again when Ralph appeared. As an obvious bribe for him to join us, we offered to buy him a drink, which he accepted. We had set about discussing the usual immaculate performance, which we had thoroughly enjoyed, when John started to criticise the understudy who had appeared for one of the principal ladies. He went on at length until said understudy appeared and made a beeline for our group. Ralph finally managed to interrupt John and said, "Have you met my wife?" Despite the horror we felt at John's gaffe, we stayed on chatting with them, but the following week, to salve our consciences, we gave her a gift at the Stage Door. After the performance, we were having a drink when we got a note from her.

"To the four fanatics in the bar, thank you so much for your company and the beautiful orchid." Embarrassing? Not half!'

The D'Oyly Carte attracted many odd characters to the front row of the theatres it played, most of whom were given nicknames by the cast, but that did not necessarily make them, in the words of W.S. Gilbert, 'pestilential nuisances who write for autographs'. Most of us who were in the company in the 1970s can remember, in particular, the London bus conductor who always turned up to watch the shows in her uniform. Known as 'Tickets', she cut a very odd figure and it was hard to tell if it was a man or a woman. However comical she appeared, she bothered no-one; she was just there. Often sitting just a few seats away was the instantly recognisable figure of Philippa Taylor, whose retirement years were almost exclusively devoted to following the D'Oyly Carte wherever it went. She cut a rather pathetic figure with her shabby clothes, shock of unruly grey hair and decaying teeth, but appearances can be deceptive. Often the butt of jokes, very few of the company members realised that she was a woman of great intellect, who had held a position of responsibility high up, it was believed, in the Civil Service, or a government department. She is known to have had numerous letters published in *The Times*, her incisive take on current affairs belying her eccentric appearance.

After every performance she attended, Philippa could be seen outside the Stage Door, quiet and unassuming, but hoping for a few words with her favourite performers. She seemed to be a permanent fixture. No-one can now remember how her relationship with John Taylor, the viola player in the D'Oyly Carte orchestra, began, but there was astonishment within the company when they got married and Philippa joined us on tour. Principal soprano, Barbara Lilley, relates that Philippa was a talented photographer and remembers being given boxed sets of beautiful photographs she had taken. When Barbara left the company expecting a baby, Philippa gave her a matinee coat and hat which she had made. So beautiful was it, that Barbara and her husband, company baritone, Peter Lyon, have kept it to this day. Long after the closure of the D'Oyly Carte, Philippa, despite failing health, continued to follow the company's performers in their G&S pursuits. She died early in 2017, having watched over eight hundred company performances, a legend in her own right.

'Bap', 'Goggles', 'Dirt and Gert', 'The Owls' and 'Eighty-Eight' were just a few of the nicknames given to the fanatical D'Oyly Carte followers who were such a feature of company life. By and large, they were generously tolerated by the performers, who signed autographs time after time and exchanged a few words with these faithful fans. Occasionally, some fans were popular with the company members and were considered as friends. 'The Owls', Ruth and Jen, fell into this category. They always sat together and got their nickname because they both wore large-framed spectacles. Everyone liked and trusted them. But how did these devotees regard each other? Diana Burleigh, who followed the company before emigrating to Australia, gives a fascinating insight into the world outside the Stage Door.

'The fans were not all one group. A few were devoted to one singer, others just loved G&S and the D'Oyly Carte, wanting to know more about the operas and their creators. I went along as a teenager to Golders Green Hippodrome, a vast theatre on the northern edge of London. I was waiting to buy a ticket for the very cheap gallery which was accessed by a long and winding flight of stairs. I met a lady called Vanessa who was a member of the Gilbert and Sullivan Society and who was a keen Carte fan without being a fanatic. I attended every night of the season and after one performance Vanessa said she was going to hang around the Stage Door to see the company leave. I joined her and discovered there was a group of regular fans there. Whenever the Carte was within striking distance of London I began attending the operas and formed friendships with other fans.

'There were always a few who went too far and most of us felt that we should respect the privacy of the company, which some breached. On the other hand, one Tom Round fan found herself on the same plane as him and her seat was between him and the lavatory. She did not want him to think she was stalking him, so she "held on" for the duration of the flight. Yes, weird!

'However, we did know all the company gossip and who was with whom. We may have discussed this among ourselves, but clammed up with outsiders. We also liked to acknowledge special occasions, when we contributed towards chocolates and flowers etc. Some of us saw off the company from the Savoy when they left for a tour of the USA. Once, we gave out several large boxes of chocolates for them to share, but in the wrapping of each box was a parody from the operas which were rather rude about the management. No-one took the blame for having written them, but we did hear they went down very well!

'In time, I got to know some members of the company and this is where the differences between fans became apparent. Some were besotted and I was cautious of being associated with them as pesterers of the performers. Nevertheless, it was always nice to get to know some of the company and chat to them. Mostly this was a casual relationship, but other encounters blossomed into friendship. For me, these friends included Mary Sansom, Gillian Humphreys and Lyndsie Holland who I kept in touch with over the years. I also valued being able to discuss performances and the productions with people I admired, including Philip Potter, Valerie Masterson, Peggy Ann Jones and Meston Reid. We, of course, attended all the special performances and had a collection of stories of the things we had seen on and off the stage. Philip Potter, as Nanki-Poo in *The Mikado*, having to shin up the tori gate to retrieve the rope noose which had got stuck when he tried to throw it over the gate, causing John Reed to collapse in laughter; Peggy Ann Jones losing a petticoat and kicking it off-stage along with her shoe; the blindfolded Thomas Round as Marco in *The Gondoliers* catching Pauline Wales as Tessa instead of Mary Sansom as Gianetta in the "My papa he keeps three horses" section, much to the panic of both ladies! Happy days!'

For all the obsessive fans, there were far more who would merely describe themselves as lovers of the D'Oyly Carte and the Savoy Operas, who attended as many performances as they could, but were not necessarily interested in meeting the stars of the company. Ann Hughes and Jill Cutler fell into this category as Ann describes.

'In the 1960s I became friendly with a nurse at the Queen Elizabeth Hospital in Birmingham, who was living in the same hospital accommodation as me. Jill was knowledgeable about Gilbert and Sullivan and on one of the D'Oyly Carte's regular visits to Birmingham, she suggested that I accompany her to the Alexandra Theatre. I loved it. Both Jill and I joined The Friends of D'Oyly Carte, receiving advanced information as to where the company would be performing. One holiday a year would be spent somewhere on the coast, or in a Scottish city, where we spent a week taking in the shows, but for the company's visits to Birmingham, we attended almost every night. During the annual London season we would go to a performance fortnightly, travelling on the 4pm "theatre train" from Birmingham, returning on the last train just after 11pm. Occasionally, we stayed for the weekend. Over the years, we collected all the D'Oyly Carte magazines and recordings – we just loved the music. Many of our friends could not understand our fascination with it all and we found it very hard to describe to those who didn't know anything about it.'

Ann and Jill's great friendship, forged from their mutual love of G&S, ended with Jill's untimely death, but the memories for Ann never fade. Their story is typical of so many whose love of the D'Oyly Carte Opera Company has enriched their lives. Valerie Bailey, a familiar figure at many a performance in the last few years of the company's life, first saw the D'Oyly Carte at the Blackpool Opera House in 1972. For a birthday present, her boyfriend bought her tickets for every opera performed and she was captivated. Prior to this, she had only ever seen the Savoy Operas at church group level. After one show, she went with her boyfriend to the Stage Door to get autographs and was thrilled when they were invited to join some of the company for a drink in the bar. She recalls how wonderful it was to feel part of the family from the start and, over the next ten years, saw many performances in theatres all over the country. Whilst living in Birmingham, she joined the local branch of the Gilbert and Sullivan Society before moving to the Manchester branch in 1977. After the D'Oyly Carte's closure in 1982, Valerie continued to follow and support its members in any Gilbert and Sullivan productions or concerts in which they were taking part, something that has continued to this day. She would be the first to admit that her passion for the Carte and its performers has been a huge part of her life. Her enthusiasm never fades and she takes great pleasure in keeping in contact with those performers she has come to consider as her friends.

For all the many anonymous fans of the company, there were many well-known figures charmed by the delights of Gilbert and Sullivan as delivered by the D'Oyly Carte. The company's music assistant, Paul Seeley, remembers the great actress, Dame Flora Robson, attending performances when the company was in Brighton and, in 1982, sending her an official company calendar specially designed to celebrate the centenary year of *Iolanthe*, featuring photographs of the cast which he had taken. Dame Flora sent him a treasured letter of thanks. In the 1970s, another famous actress, Judi Dench, now also a Dame, took the opportunity to look in on a matinee of *The Mikado* whilst she was rehearsing a production in Stratford-upon-Avon. Stage Manager, Ken Robertson-Scott, was running the corner for the performance and remembers his surprise when she quietly approached him and, quite properly, asked his permission to watch the show from the wings. After about half an hour, during which time she had laughed in delight at the antics on the stage, she whispered her thanks and told him she had better get back to her rehearsal, although would have preferred to stay to see the whole show, which she thought wonderful, remarking to Ken how much she admired the company's great theatrical heritage.

On the other side of the Atlantic, the popular science fiction writer, Isaac Asimov, was well-known for his love of G&S and the D'Oyly Carte. He was a long-term member of the Gilbert and Sullivan Society of New York, regularly attending their monthly meetings and contributing to the activities of the group. He was also a supporter of the New York Gilbert and Sullivan Players and endowed an award given annually to a company member for their service. Asimov would have been well-acquainted with another member of the Gilbert and Sullivan Society of New York, Jesse Sherreff. Jesse and his wife, Rochelle, were ardent fans of the D'Oyly Carte and were very popular with the company performers. Whenever the Carte was playing in New York, they would host legendary parties for the cast. Jesse had two huge collections of which he was very proud. One was of G&S and D'Oyly Carte memorabilia and the other of pornography, of which he had made a serious study. No wonder he was such a popular character! Principal tenor, Geoffrey Shovelton, retained a great friendship with Jesse and Rochelle until Geoff's death and I looked forward to seeing them whenever visiting the Gilbert and Sullivan Society of New York. Ken Sandford held them in the highest esteem, always enjoying their company and generous hospitality. Sadly, Jesse recently passed away. He was a larger-than-life character who will be very much missed. He and his wife were the perfect example of the enduring bond that could exist between performers and fans.

Peter Riley, who first joined the D'Oyly Carte as Baggage Master in 1964, progressing through stage management to eventually become Company Manager, a position he held until the demise of the company, often had to host celebrity visitors to a performance. Sometimes it was members of the Royal Family, or well-known politicians but, on one occasion, he recalls the legendary England cricketer, Sir Colin Cowdrey being in the audience.

'Sir Colin brought his son to see a matinee of *HMS Pinafore* at Sadler's Wells and came round to see me afterwards, as we had previously met. It turned out that his son, Christopher, if I remember correctly, was due to appear in a school production of *Pinafore*. He paid a second visit one evening, when James Conroy-Ward was on for John Reed, and subsequently wrote to me to say what a good "twelfth man" James was. We kept in touch after this.' Peter recalls frequently receiving letters from fans with suggestions and, sometimes, loopy ideas which all went on file and are, probably, he believes, in the D'Oyly Carte archive now held by the British Library.

A radio presenter who had from childhood been an ardent D'Oyly Carte fan, Ed Doolan, for many years used his shows on BBC Radio WM to indulge his passion by interviewing the principals whenever the company was appearing in Birmingham. Attending as many performances as possible during a two-week season at the Alexandra Theatre was never enough for Ed; he wanted to sit opposite his favourite G&S stars in the intimacy of his studio, chatting with them as old friends. Ostensibly to promote the D'Oyly Carte's profile and encourage the good folk of Brum to see its shows, Ed's interviews were a thinly-veiled excuse to spend time with the performers he so admired.

As a political journalist, Ed Doolan interviewed all the big guns, from Nelson Mandela to Margaret Thatcher, his tough interviewing style earning him respect from every quarter. An appearance on his show was both welcomed and dreaded: he took no prisoners. However, sitting across the microphone from D'Oyly Carters turned him into a pussy cat as he prompted the interviewees, then sat back and enjoyed himself, quietly chuckling at their stories. On more than one occasion, he persuaded his BBC bosses to fund a two-hour special to be broadcast during the Christmas period. With the likes of John Ayldon, Patricia

Leonard, John Reed and Kenneth Sandford amongst others, Ed knew he could guarantee his listeners an entertaining time, whilst he was like a schoolboy in a sweet shop. Could he ever have imagined that the Australian lad, whose mother had introduced him to the delights of Gilbert and Sullivan via the recordings of the D'Oyly Carte, would find himself on the other side of the world in the presence of the people whose voices had enchanted him for so long?

Although Ed was passionate about the D'Oyly Carte, he was even more passionate about Gilbert and Sullivan. Whenever an amateur group had an upcoming G&S production in the West Midlands area, he would plug it on his programme and encourage his audience to go and see it. He attended as many amateur G&S shows as his busy schedule permitted. He once sang King Gama's song, "If you give me your attention", from *Princess Ida*, live on air and made an excellent job of it. I know, because I was in the studio at the time. Ed was a long-standing friend and I have done many an interview on his radio show, but that didn't stop him from wickedly tossing me an unexpectedly awkward question and then watch me struggle as he grinned at me over the microphone. Ed was a true fan, who used his professional position to promote The D'Oyly Carte Opera Company and its Gilbert and Sullivan heritage whenever he could. His death in 2018 robbed us of a truly remarkable man.

Another fan of the company to have given as much to the cause of Gilbert and Sullivan as he took from it was Ian G. Smith. Director of the International Gilbert and Sullivan Festival, which he founded with the help of his son, Neil, it is now in its twenty-seventh year. Ian was the brains behind its enormous success. Bringing together G&S fans from around the world for two weeks each year to celebrate the Savoy Operas and perpetuate the memory of the D'Oyly Carte, Ian's brainchild is spawning another generation of G&S lovers. His own introduction to the D'Oyly Carte was down to a very special lady.

'You might say it was my mother who changed my life. She was the star of our local church Gilbert and Sullivan Society and when they organised a group visit to Manchester to see the D'Oyly Carte, she invited me to tag along. I have been tagging along ever since – for nearly seventy years! I will swear that Thomas Round sang 'Take a Pair of Sparkling Eyes', from *The Gondoliers*, just for me and I am sure that

60

Valerie Masterson picked me out in the audience for whatever love song she was singing that evening. I found it pure magic and would never have believed that, one day, Tom, Valerie, Ken Sandford, Peggy Ann Jones, Gillian Knight, John Ayldon, Patricia Leonard and Geoffrey Shovelton would sing in my opera company.

'From the age of sixteen I was playing the "patter parts" in my mother's church group. Whenever I could, I was watching John Reed perform them. With my libretto on my knee I am sure I noted every time he blinked. And when the conductor, Isidore Godfrey, cut an encore at a matinee, I wanted to ask for my money back! I could never have dreamt that John Reed would end up trying to buy my house in Huddersfield. He eventually moved to Halifax and directed the amateur group I had founded in the 1970s, when I was privileged to have him direct me in so many of the famous roles he had made his own. There is no doubt how much he loved his G&S. Shortly before he died, I went to visit him, leaving my son, Henry, in the car. John was slumped in a chair looking very ill. I asked if I could bring Henry in, as he was playing Reginald Bunthorne in the festival youth production of *Patience*, in the hope that John might help him with some of the dialogue. His reaction was what I expected – or at least hoped. His eyes opened, he was lively and alert. "Not like that – like this!" In five minutes he had shed twenty years and I remember thinking, "Lucky Henry". There will never be another John Reed.

'I was more than angry when it was announced that the D'Oyly Carte was closing, with lots of rumours about bad management and unnecessary costs. I never saw them in London, only in Manchester, Leeds, Bradford and, occasionally, in Nottingham, but the audience always felt like family and when we started our own Gilbert and Sullivan Festival, I wanted it to feel exactly the same. I would like to think it does and this is thanks, in no small measure, to the fantastic support we received from the "original" D'Oyly Carte stars who were happy to discover a new G&S life rubbing shoulders with, and delighting, their fans. Thanks, Mum. Without your enthusiasm I might never have met my heroes, Mr Gilbert and his mate, Mr Sullivan!'

This contribution from Ian G. Smith was made before he died in November, 2019. Ian did so much to promote the works of Gilbert and Sullivan through his annual festivals in Buxton and Harrogate, for which we owe him a debt of gratitude. They were a labour of love. Thanks, Ian; the festival won't be the same without you.

As has already been mentioned, D'Oyly Carte fans came in all sorts of packaging, some of them rather larger than life. In 1997, Robert Gawthrop was delighted to learn that the International Gilbert and Sullivan Festival would be coming to Philadelphia. An ardent G&S man, he regularly appeared with amateur troupes in the greater Philadelphia area and was a stalwart of the Savoy Company, the oldest amateur Gilbert and Sullivan group in the world. For many years, he had appeared in the 'Pooh-Bah' baritone roles for the famous old company and his hero was Kenneth Sandford, the holder of those parts in the D'Oyly Carte Opera Company. Although he had briefly met Ken at a G&S symposium held in West Chester, Pennsylvania, in the late 1980s, the possibility of once again meeting the man whose voice he had come to love from the D'Oyly Carte recordings he had collected was very exciting. Rob, as he was known to his friends, indeed did meet Ken again and was thrilled to see him perform in the flesh, as 'Sir Despard Murgatroyd' in *Ruddigore* and 'Captain Corcoran' in *HMS Pinafore*. Never what could be called the shy, retiring type, Rob had asked me to introduce him to Ken. I had directed Rob as the 'Pirate King' in *The Pirates of Penzance* as part of the very first Gilbert and Sullivan Festival in Buxton in 1994 and we became friends. I duly brought the pair together and, as they chatted after a performance, Rob told Ken that he had enjoyed seeing him at work and invited his idol to come to watch him at work. Ever the gentleman, Ken agreed and a date was fixed.

It was with some trepidation that Ken went through the security screening at the federal courthouse in downtown Philadelphia and slipped self-consciously into the public gallery, quickly finding a seat and hoping no-one had noticed his entry in the middle of a trial. He had every right to be nervous, because the judge, a huge man of six feet four inches, looked very intimidating sat high up on his bench swathed in a black robe. The Honorable Robert Smith Gawthrop III was hearing a murder trial. To Ken's astonishment, His Honour immediately spoke and asked the gentleman who had just entered his court to stand and name himself. Probably the only time in his career that Kenneth Sandford had stuttered over two words, he did as he was told, turning crimson with embarrassment. Glad to be able to sit down again, he soon immersed himself in the intricacies of the legal proceedings. But more fun was to follow. The judge, who was questioning one of the defendants about the shooting of a shopkeeper, suddenly burst into song: "Who fired that shot? At once the truth declare." This line, sung by 'The Lieutenant of the Tower' to 'Wilfred Shadbolt' in *The Yeomen of the Guard*, was, of course, very familiar to Ken, who played 'Shadbolt' for the D'Oyly Carte. The unexpected singing reduced Ken to stifled hysteria as the incongruity of the situation hit home, not helped by the self-satisfied smirk on the face of the judge. It took him some time to regain his composure, but that surreal moment was one of Ken's favourite stories. Unlikely, you may think, far-fetched? Quite true: I was also sitting in the court room.

Of course, not every fan was as memorably eccentric as the inimitable Rob Gawthrop. It is probably fair to say that D'Oyly Carters always thought that G&S seems to attract cranks, but surely this is true of any particular passion, hobby or interest? In truth, the vast majority of the company's fans were ordinary folk who loved the words and music of the Savoy Operas and enjoyed a visit to the theatre. That such people had done the same since the 1870s attests to the enduring qualities of the works of Gilbert and Sullivan. For all the musical snobs who think that G&S is just 'rumpty-tumpty stuff', perhaps they should take a closer look. Millions of people are, surely, not all wrong. As my friend, the eminent musician and Elgar scholar, Dr Donald Hunt, OBE, once said to me, 'If it was good enough for Sir Edward Elgar, it's good enough for everyone else.'

CHAPTER FOUR

AND ON THE OTHER HAND ...

The affection, devotion and even love shown to the principals of the D'Oyly Carte Opera Company by their fans may have been flattering, but it was rarely mutual. Stage Door attentions were a part of the job and the performers dealt with them, in most cases, with good grace. Professionalism was the name of the game. However tired, or anxious to get away after a show, they stopped to chat and sign programmes, sometimes posing for photographs when not looking at their best. This could take quite a time when there was a throng waiting for a glimpse of their idols. Naturally, the great names of the company were targeted more than the less well-known principals, a brief chat with them being the greatest prize of all. Whilst the leading artistes were doing what they had to, the members of the chorus were able to slip away unnoticed, as if they had played no part in the performance, their minor contribution seldom considered worthy of an autograph. That is how it was, and it was accepted. For the most part, relations between performers and fans were cordial and good-natured, but there were exceptions, when fanatics crossed the line of decent behaviour in pursuit of their quarry.

John Reed, so often the target of adoring fans, was always coy about revealing his age. Towards the end of his D'Oyly Carte career, he was very conscious of having to play the part of a young man in some of the operas, such as 'Robin Oakapple' in *Ruddigore* or 'Jack Point' in *The Yeomen of the Guard*. However good his make-up, he knew that he was getting past looking youthful. Like many comedians, he had his insecurities and getting older was one of them. Kenneth Sandford, another veteran, often recalled the humorous exchanges between them about their advancing years. But that was for them in the privacy of the dressing room. As earlier mentioned by Diana Burleigh, a fan went to the considerable trouble of acquiring an official copy of John's birth certificate to bring to an end the fans' speculation as to how old he was. When he found out that proof of his age had been circulated amongst the faithful at the Stage Door, he was incandescent with rage and terribly hurt. John loved his loyal fans, spending hours reading their letters, and the thought that one of them had done such an unkind thing upset him very much. It is probably true to say that he never felt quite the same about the fans again, particularly as he never found out which of them was responsible. He felt betrayed and his trust in them had gone. It took him a long time to get over such an unnecessary prank.

John Reed's popularity during his long D'Oyly Carte career brought him into contact with fans from all over the world, their adoration of his talent sometimes driving them to extraordinary lengths to have a word with him. Chorus baritone and understudy, Bruce Graham, recalls the amusing occasion when he and John were walking along the Strand after a performance at the Savoy Theatre, being pursued by a fan who kept calling out to him. Anxious not to get involved when on his way home, John took a desperate measure to avoid the fan who was rapidly catching up with them. Having hurriedly explained to Bruce what he was about to do, John hailed a taxi that he didn't need and jumped into it, driving a short distance before telling the driver to stop so that he could walk back to where he needed to be. A costly measure no doubt, but the famous patter man did what he had to do.

The well-loved principal tenor, Meston Reid, was another to suffer spiteful behaviour at the hands of a fan, as principal mezzo-soprano, Jane Metcalfe relates.

'We were in Wolverhampton and between shows, for some reason, I was in John Ayldon's dressing room, chatting with he and Guy Matthews. Meston came in with a ham sandwich which, he said, had just been delivered to him at the Stage Door by a fan. We all laughed at the implication of hammy acting but, ever the innocent, Meston hadn't seen the joke, which was a bit cruel, but we had!'

The constant attentions of some of the fans could be a nuisance to the principals, but it was not unknown for an obsession to have a slightly sinister undertone. As John Reed's understudy, James Conroy-Ward had to live with the fact that he was not popular with all of the fans. Being the man that nobody wanted to see was a heavy burden to carry, a load made heavier by the unwanted attentions of two very strange ladies who often tracked his movements. Nicknamed 'Dirt and Gert' by the company members, the two fat women were no oil paintings who always looked rather greasy and unkempt. Never known to smile, there was something slightly threatening about their presence outside the Stage Door. James remembers that they seemed displeased when he didn't speak to them, but never responded when he did. They unnerved him and he dreaded seeing their white van, which had a large mouth with protruding red tongue painted on the side of it.

One night, during a season at the Manchester Opera House, he came out of the Stage Door, acknowledged the two women, then began walking to Deansgate Station to catch a train home. He noticed that they were slowly following him in the van and he was glad to get inside the station. To his dismay, when he got off the train at Timperley, they were parked outside the station and tracked him to his mother's house. Not long after this unsettling incident, the women were once again outside the theatre when James emerged. Rather than walk to the station with them following, he hailed a taxi, but the distinctive van was soon in pursuit. Feeling as if he was in some strange film, he explained his situation to the cab driver and asked him to 'lose the white van'. By the time the taxi was nearing Timperley, the van was just out of sight, so the driver pulled over, turned on the 'for hire' light and told James to get down on the back seat so they would think he had got out. As the van and its fooled occupants drove past, the cabby waited a moment and then delivered James safely to his doorstep.

James admits that these strange women intimidated him, because he did not know what motivated them, or what else they might do. He soon found out; they changed tack. Out of the blue, they sent him a picture postcard of the Eastbourne College of Domestic Science, where his wife, Shirley, had studied. If anything, this shook him even more, because he had no idea how they could know this, no more than how they found out where he lived in Wimbledon, or where his mother lived in Timperley. It must be supposed that 'Dirt and Gert' eventually tired of their machinations, but James has never forgotten how much their shenanigans worried him.

Obsessive D'Oyly Carte fans were not uncommon, but such extreme tactics as James encountered were. For men to be infatuated with an attractive young lady they saw on the D'Oyly Carte stage would have happened throughout the company's history. The Oscar-winning film, *Chariots of Fire*, portrays the 1924 Olympic athlete, Harold Abrahams, falling for the D'Oyly Carte's principal soprano, Sybil Gordon, at a performance of *The Mikado*. In reality, Abrahams was never engaged to Sybil Gordon, but actually married another company performer, mezzo-soprano Sybil Evers. Despite this artistic licence, the point is made: men and women often fall in love with people they see on the stage, a fantasy rarely fulfilled.

In the late 1950s, soprano Vera Ryan was shopping in a large store in Newcastle when she realised that she was being followed around by a man who could not take his eyes off her, which she found rather uncomfortable.

'Then I received a fan letter addressed to "the fourth contadine on the right". There was no further encounter as I was preparing a wedding – mine to Alan! If the letter was from the stalker – too unkind a word perhaps – then I missed out. He was gorgeous!' The man concerned had obviously seen Vera in *The Gondoliers* and liked what he saw, but his charms were not enough to dissuade her from marrying the love of her life, principal baritone and legendary D'Oyly Carte matinee idol, Alan Styler. Alan was used to the attention of adoring female fans. Handsome and charming, with a wicked sense of humour, he was a firm favourite with the ladies. A principal soprano in the 1950s, Cynyhia Morey remembers the story of him being approached by a lady at the Stage Door who commented that he had lovely legs.

Alan's self-effacing reply was to say that he had left them hanging up in the dressing room! Having seen him wearing tights, the adoring fan would have had no idea that Alan was actually wearing calf enhancers because his legs were so thin.

Another young D'Oyly Carte lady of the 1950s, who shall remain nameless to spare her blushes, was very flattered by the letters written to her by an admirer. Young and naïve, she accepted the gifts he sent, which included a bolt of cloth for her to have a dress made, and a necklace. Eventually, she agreed to go out to dinner with him after a performance in Manchester. An older, obviously wealthy man, he turned up at the Stage Door in a Rolls Royce Silver Cloud. After the meal, he asked her if she had ever been to Jodrell Bank. After telling him she had not, she was whisked away to see the famous radio telescope in the dark. The obvious consequences left her fighting to make sure her reputation remained unsullied. One can't blame a man for trying his luck.

For company principals, in particular, fan letters were an everyday occurrence. Usually posted to the Stage Door, they were always avidly read. What artiste doesn't enjoy an ego massage? Principal contralto, Christene Palmer, still has a letter from 1973 sent to her by an American fan who had heard her singing of "There Grew a Little Flower" from *Ruddigore* on a compilation recording. He was enraptured by her performance, which he thought the best ever of the touching piece, so the letter still means a great deal to her. The great stars of the D'Oyly Carte received fan mail aplenty and most of them tried to reply to as many letters as possible, although this was not always practical. Sometimes, friendships that lasted for many years were formed from an exchange of correspondence. The popular principal mezzo-soprano, Lorraine Daniels, had a fan called Gerald Benson, with whom she exchanged letters and Christmas cards for many years. He frequently went to Moscow on business and always brought back a gift for her. From Russia with love, doubtless.

Principal contralto, Gillian Knight, still has a letter written to her in 1961 from the impresario, Raymond Gubbay, which he penned when he was just fifteen years old, as she tells us:

'In it he raves about a performance of *Mikado* at the Savoy and says that "the company need have no fear of competition from a certain theatre in the Haymarket whose players can neither sing nor act well, and where the music and words were so altered that it's a cheek to call them Gilbert and Sullivan!" I wonder what he thinks now?'

A D'Oyly Carte fan from childhood, Raymond attended performances whenever he could and, having become a successful impresario, included G&S in his programmes long after the company folded, doing much to keep the Savoy Operas in the public eye.

Melissa Sinden Grey, daughter of tenor, Frederick Sinden and mezzo-soprano, Beryl Dixon, both company members in the 1950s, relates that her mother and father both had fans who were ardent admirers.

'I know Mum still has a lovely little china figurine from a gentleman fan who wrote regularly to her. The piece arrived with a note saying that he couldn't write any more as he was getting engaged and his fiancée didn't understand! Then there was another guy who wrote her weird poems. My dad kept a couple of saucy fan letters from some ladies – but that was Fred for you! And they made some great life-long friends who started out as fans.'

The arrival of a fan letter from a German lady to James-Conroy Ward was the start of an intriguing correspondence between the two. He first met her in Norwich when the company was playing at the Theatre Royal and she spoke to him outside the theatre. James remembers that she particularly admired his 'Major-General' in *The Pirates of Penzance*, which he played in his own right when he was understudy to John Reed. When he took over from John as principal comedian, the lady continued to regularly write to him and send him books that she had written. He would, of course, reply to thank her and there seemed to be a friendship developing between them. Intrigued to know more about her background, as she seemed to be a woman of great intellect, he was curious to know how a lady from Germany came to be such a fan of Gilbert and Sullivan. He eventually wrote and asked her more about herself, after which he never heard from her again. Convinced he must have offended her, he was rather saddened by the abrupt end to their correspondence. Her name was Leni Riefenstahl.

At the time, the name meant nothing to him but, sometime later, he tried to find out more about her and was absolutely astounded to discover that she was a close and trusted friend of Adolph

Hitler. Her astonishing CV showed her to be a dancer, actress, film director, producer, photographer and author of international acclaim. Impressed by the films she had made, the Nazi leader is believed to have approached her to collaborate on propaganda films and the two became friends. There are many photographs of her filming important occasions in the presence of Hitler and other high-ranking Nazi officials. Perhaps her best-known work nowadays is the famous footage she shot at the 1936 Olympic Games in Berlin, which featured the four-time American gold medallist, Jesse Owens.

It is hardly surprising James was shocked that such a famous, or as some may consider her, infamous, woman should be a devotee of Gilbert and Sullivan and a fan of his performances. That she wrote to him and sent him her books seems surreal to him now. However, at my behest, he has mounted a long-overdue clear-out of his loft, turning up two of her books but, alas, no letters which might have been included here. Who would have thought it?

A somewhat less controversial correspondent was an obsessive fan of principal soprano, Mary Sansom, according to her husband and fellow D'Oyly Carter, Alan Barrett. The fan, a lady who lived in Australia, frequently wrote letters to Mary and asked for signed photographs. Mary duly obliged, but it was more than thirty years later, long after the company had closed down, that the true extent of the fan's fixation became apparent. Alan and Mary were at the International Gilbert and Sullivan Festival in Buxton and, to their surprise, so was her fan. When they actually met, she had with her all the many photographs she had collected of Mary over the years, including all those which had been signed! Such devotion may have been flattering, but no-one could deny that it was odd.

In 1970, a fan letter of a different kind was sent to the company by an elderly lady offering afternoon tea to any company members who would care to visit her for a chat. Chorus ladies, Jacqui Veazey and Joan Hedley volunteered to go and were given the address by the company Stage Manager, Peter Riley. Jacqui recalls that it was anything but the pleasant experience they were expecting.

'The house stank of urine and the afternoon tea consisted of toasted teacakes which were stale and hard and undrinkable tea. When our hostess went out to get more tea, Joan and I took the opportunity to wrap the inedible cakes in paper serviettes and stuff them into our handbags so as not to offend her, before pouring our tea into plant pots!' That old soul obviously meant well, but the joys of D'Oyly Carte fans were sometimes very dubious, not least at the Stage Door, where obtaining prized autographs was a serious and, sometimes, brutal business. Principal baritone, Clive Harré, still bridles at the rudeness of one fan, as he relates.

'I very rarely got asked to sign an autograph, mainly because no-one ever recognised me. The reason for this being that I wore a ginger wig in *Pirates*, I looked like Henry VIII in *Yeomen*, I stuck on large whiskers for *Pinafore* and with my "old" make-up, I didn't even recognise myself in *The Sorcerer*. One evening, I came out of the Stage Door at Sadler's Wells Theatre in London and a lady stepped forward, fluttering her programme in front of my face. She asked me to sign it but, as I went to take it, she pulled it away and had the cheek to ask if I was a principal, a member of the chorus, or orchestra. This rather took me aback and I inexplicably said that I was in the chorus, to which she replied, "Oh, sorry, I don't want yours," and whipped the programme from under my nose! I was flabbergasted and angry that she was so insensitive, storming off to get the tube with a look of thunder on my face.'

For the chorus members, this behaviour was usual. From my own point of view, when I was playing a role in *The Mikado*, *HMS Pinafore* or *The Pirates of Penzance*, I was often asked for my autograph or a photograph, but the same fans who asked me to sign their programmes would not bother with me the following night if it had been a show in which I was on the back row. This snobbery did little to make choristers feel valued as performers and one can only wonder if these people were bothered about the many glorious choruses written by Sir Arthur Sullivan. If they did, then why not admire the singers who performed them? We were certainly made to feel second-class artistic citizens by the fans jostling around the principals as we left the theatre unnoticed. Similarly, when understudies went on, they suddenly became important to the fans for taking a principal role, but their signatures were requested only for as long as they were deputising. As soon as they returned to chorus duties they became invisible again. It was usually the same at social functions hosted by local operatic societies or golf clubs anxious to entertain the D'Oyly Carte Opera Company. When drawn into conversation and asked what part you had taken, as soon as it was apparent you were in the chorus, excuses were made to move away. It didn't matter; we were used to it, but Kenneth Sandford was once left speechless by a lady at a function hosted by Hull G&S Society. When asked what part he had played, he told her he was 'Pooh-Bah'. 'Oh, you play my husband's roles.'

Some fans were, seemingly, unaware that they could be rather rude, or abrupt. Barbara Lilley, as down-to-earth a person as you could ever meet, was never interested in being seen as a glamorous principal soprano with a famous opera company; it was not her style, and Jane Metcalfe clearly remembers an amusing encounter Barbara had with a tactless fan.

'We were playing the Forum in Billingham and it was Barbara's, Geoff Shovelton's and my second venue after joining. Barbara was renowned for not being concerned about looking the part of a 'diva' off-stage. After a matinee she went out of the Stage Door, hair scraped back, to get some air, looking somewhat different from her stage persona. A fan said to her, "Is Barbara Lilley coming out soon?" Barbara replied, "I'm Barbara Lilley," to which came the response, "Oh, I thought you were the cleaner."' How typical of Barbara that she still sees the funny side of that exchange.

Hanging around the Stage Door waiting for a glimpse of favourite D'Oyly Carte performers and, hopefully, having a few words with them, was what many of the ardent company fans loved to do. It was a harmless pastime which brought them great pleasure and seldom bothered the objects of their passion. But there were always some who never knew where to draw the line, as Clive Harré recounts.

'Whenever the company was on tour in places close to London, like Brighton, I would rent a flat and my wife, Jeanette, came to join me. This always pleased Meston Reid, who was having trouble with two ladies who were besotted with him. When he left the Stage Door, they would keep touching him and follow him to his car, which he hated. In an attempt to stop them, if he knew that Jeanette was in the theatre, he would make a bee-line for her and it became her job to escort him from the theatre, walking hand-in-hand with him to his car, where she would kiss him on the cheek and wave him off. She would then return to the theatre to collect me, by which time the two ladies had disappeared with a look of discomfort on their faces.'

The efforts of some fans to become closely associated with D'Oyly Carte principals sometimes bordered on obsessive, their attentions often causing considerable nuisance. Kenneth Sandford was plagued for many years by a middle-aged lady who showered him with gifts and thought nothing of turning up on the doorstep of his Ealing home late at night bearing a cake she had made for him. His wife, Pauline, and daughter, Mandy, still remember with amusement the lengths that the fan, whose name was Anne, went to in order to become his friend. They recall her as a respectable and well-dressed married woman, rather matronly in appearance, who would have looked more at home at the Women's Institute than waiting outside the Stage Door of London's Sadler's Wells Theatre for a brief chat with her hero. That she was generous was undisputed, but Ken sometimes struggled to be patient with her when her attentions became too intrusive.

Mandy and Pauline also remember her being a very creative and artistic person, whose intricately decorated cakes might be topped off by a marzipan figure of 'Pooh-Bah' or 'Sir Despard Murgatroyd'. She crafted beautiful hand-painted eggs in the style of Fabergé to give him and spent what must have been many hours making detailed models of all of Ken's characters, complete with authentic miniature costumes. So good were they, that they still take pride of place in Pauline's display cabinet. Anne was a familiar figure during the company's London seasons, but the mind boggles as to how she found the time and money to attend so many D'Oyly Carte performances when she was believed to have a similar passion for the actor, Sir Derek Jacobi, and Irish snooker legend, Alex 'Hurricane' Higgins. I can remember Ken saying it was rumoured that her long-suffering husband took to the bottle.

For all the instances of inconvenience, or upset, caused by over-enthusiastic fans, most were respectful, kind and considerate; they were also useful on occasion, even feeding parking meters between shows to save the artistes having to get out of costume and make-up to do it themselves. The hugely-popular mezzo-soprano, Peggy Ann Jones says she could always bank on a prompt from the front row if she forgot her words. But then, Jane Metcalfe would say to the contrary.

'I once had a bad moment during a matinee of *Yeomen* at Sadler's Wells. I sang the whole of "Were I Thy Bride" to "La, la la", doing all the actions but unable to recall any words, with both Ken Sandford, as 'Shadbolt', and Royston Nash, in the pit, staring wildly at me like rabbits frozen in headlights! I went out of the Stage Door, head down, when a fan stepped out and said, "That was a fantastic performance today" without a trace of sarcasm in her voice. She really meant it. So much for the fans knowing all the words.'

In truth, lots of the fans did know all of the words and music, down to the last comma and semi-quaver rest, only too happy to bring any minute deviation from the libretto or score to the attention of a performer guilty of making a small mistake. There was nothing more off-putting than seeing someone on the front row with their nose buried in the score of the show, sometimes shaking their head and silently 'tut-tutting' at any error. Fortunately, such sticklers for detail were few, but Harold Sharples, principal tenor for a year in 1980, remembers one lady who took attention to detail very seriously.

'I think her name was Kate. A lady of about thirty years old, she used to come to every London performance with her mother and also attended performances in Manchester and other towns whenever she could. At first, I found it odd that she watched the show with pencil poised above a notebook, periodically scribbling down something that caught her attention. After the performance, she would consult her notebook and let me know if I had made an error, or deviated in the slightest from set moves. I got used to this and it amused me to try and catch her out by putting in a different gesture, or marginally moving from my usual position. I remember on one occasion when I was playing Nanki-Poo in *Mikado*, I was in the middle of "A Wand'ring Minstrel" singing "To lay aloft in a howling breeze", when I was supposed to throw up my right hand in a gesture towards an imaginary sail. I decided on this occasion to direct the gesture towards the stage and wondered if Kate would notice. Sure enough, after the performance, she checked her notes and informed me of the change I had made. Try as I might, I don't think I ever caught her out. But she was not the only one who spotted my little variations. The Assistant Director, Jimmie Marsland, he of the eagle eye and elephantine memory of everyone's moves, would approach me with a look of puzzlement on his face. "What did you do that for?"'

Cynthia Morey and Joyce Wright in a publicity photograph prior to the 1955 tour of North America. How very quaint!

On that American tour, Joyce and Cynthia are joined by Ann Drummond-Grant and Muriel Harding

*Thomas Round, Jennifer Toye, Kenneth Sandford and Peggy Ann Jones
photographed for the Winnipeg Tribune in 1962*

Pauline Wales arriving at the Stage Door of the Wimbledon Theatre, captured by D'Oyly Carte fan, David Edwards around 1967

Donald Adams going to work, also taken by David Edwards

*Valerie Masterson
with a lovely smile for David
Edwards' camera*

*Conductor, Isidore Godfrey,
posing for David's album*

*Christene Palmer and
Assistant Music Director,
William Cowley,
snapped by David*

*Princess Ida's trusty
guards are myself and Beti
Lloyd-Jones (top)
with Anne Egglestone
and Patricia Rea*

In a scene from the 1975 centenary production of Utopia Limited are Guy Matthews, Barry Clark, Thomas Scholey and Jon Ellison

John Ayldon is the Pirate King being arrested on Blackpool beach by policemen Bryan Secombe, Alan Rice, Clive Birch and Bruce Graham

We're on the telly! Me, Barbara Lilley and Lorraine Daniels
as the Three Little Maids broadcast in Brisbane in 1979

Michael Buchan, Patricia Leonard and John Reed
on a publicity cruise in Ottawa in 1978

*Another publicity cruise that year was in San Francisco,
with my good self and John Reed*

*Robin Wilson with his father,
D'Oyly Carte trustee, Lord
Wilson of Rievaulx, the two
G&S fans pictured outside
Keble College, Oxford*

*Thomas Scholey and
Alan Spencer in the
regal surroundings of
Windsor Castle's Garter
Throne Room before the
Royal Command Performance
of HMS Pinafore in 1977*

*A windy day on the fire
escape at Sadler's Wells
Theatre courtesy of Michael
Buchan, Paul Burrows,
Gareth Jones and Barry Clark.
Boys will be boys!*

Cruising on the Norfolk Broads are Jill Pert, Beti Lloyd-Jones with her dog, Casilda, Alan Spencer and Meston Reid at the front

Golf was always a popular pastime with D'Oyly Carte folk, but not all of them were hotshots. Kenneth Sandford and Beti Lloyd-Jones seem to have lost something!

Suzanne O'Keeffe and Patricia Rea celebrating the end of the 1976 tour of North America. Well, that's one way of doing it!

Gordon Mackenzie, Beti Lloyd-Jones and James Conroy-Ward distancing themselves from Kenneth Sandford and Geoffrey Shovelton vying to be the worst-dressed tourist at Sea World, San Diego, in 1978

Poolside fun in Hollywood, with Ken Robertson-Scott, Richard Mitchell, Bryan Secombe and Michael Farran-Lee doing little to save Vivian Tierney

More poolside fun, this time in San Diego. Billy Strachan and James Conroy-Ward standing, with Ken Robertson-Scott, Meston Reid and John Reed sharing the sun bed

We must be in Australia!
James Conroy-Ward, Beti
Lloyd-Jones and Gordon
Mackenzie encounter a friendly
kangaroo in Tidbinbilla Nature
Reserve in 1979

Never invite D'Oyly Carters to a wine tasting!
Jane Stanford, Alan Spencer, John Coe-Roper, Jill Pert,
Meston Reid, Elizabeth Denham and me at a winery near Perth

In Auckland, Meston Reid and James Conroy-Ward are doing their impersonations of Leonard Osborn much to the amusement of Thomas Scholey, Susan Cochrane, John Ayldon and Guy Matthews

The Last Night of a London season was an opportunity to let loose. Here is Kenneth Sandford waiting to go on as John Travolta in a rock version of 'The Magnet and the Churn' from Patience in the late 1970s

*In another send-up of
Patience, John Reed
played Reginald Bunthorne
as a punk rocker!*

*Patience was certainly popular. Here we see Barbara Lilley leading the dance
class as char ladies in 'I cannot tell what this love may be'. Well, why not?*

The Last Night of the 1981 London season saw the dancing girls strutting their stuff as American sailors in a swing version of the peers' chorus from Iolanthe

And finally, your author about to appear in a 1920s version of 'Climbing Over Rocky Mountain' from The Pirates of Penzance, around 1977. What fun those Last Nights were!

For all their little foibles, the encouragement of fans after a bad day at the office could dispel gloom in a moment. When principal contralto, Christene Palmer, was feeling low after a show in which she felt she had not been at her best, her first thought was for the people who had paid good money to see it; they deserved the best she could give. But, invariably, when she left the theatre, the smiling fans telling her how much they had enjoyed her performance lifted her spirits and made her believe she had not been as bad as she thought. She was always very grateful for that comfort. But not all fans needed to hang around outside the Stage Door to get close to their heroes.

Life-long D'Oyly Carte fan, Peter Parker, became a devotee of the company by default. His father started work for the D'Oyly Carte, on the managerial side, at the Savoy Hotel in 1913, so the young Peter was steeped in the company's affairs from as early as he could remember, learning much about Gilbert and Sullivan from Grahame Clifford, who played the comic baritone parts during the Second World War years. He was also privy to company affairs, such as the long-term contract offered to Thomas Round as an inducement for him to leave Sadler's Wells Opera Company and return to the D'Oyly Carte with security of employment. Artistes' contracts were usually renewed on an annual basis, but Peter knew that the management, having persuaded Tom to return to the company, had offered a contract in excess of two years, thought to be a first for the company, which was kept secret from other principals.

As a youngster, Peter sometimes joined his family on tour dates and can remember having a wonderful time on a golf course in Aberdeen, caddying for the likes of Darrell Fancourt and Richard Watson. He was privileged to watch the shows from the wings, absorbing the music and productions, under caution from the Stage Manager not to make any noise. Some years later, in the 1940s, he joined his parents for the D'Oyly Carte Christmas season at the Memorial Theatre in Stratford-upon-Avon, staying with company members at The Old Swan. It produced one memorable, if slightly embarrassing, opportunity to make himself useful.

'One evening, probably a Sunday, all the lights in the hotel fused and a cry was heard, "Send for Peter Parker!" It was known I was doing my electrical engineering apprenticeship in Birmingham, so

I fixed the fuse as there was nobody on duty in the hotel to do that kind of thing. About ten minutes later it all fused again, so I put in a stronger fuse. It then happened at least twice more, by which time I was getting suspicious. I was a naïve teenager, but I soon found out that it was deliberate. Someone was putting a coin into a lamp-holder, then switching on the light, causing the fuse to blow. It was then pointed out to me that with no lights on in the hotel, it could not be discovered who was in what bedroom! I became educated.'

Peter was in an unusual position: he was a D'Oyly Carte fan from within the company, loving everything about G&S, whilst having access to the intimate life of the company that most of its followers would envy. He remembers being at parties at Grimsdyke (the home of W.S. Gilbert). One was to mark the retirement of the long-serving wardrobe mistress, Cis Blain. Owner of the company, Bridget D'Oyly Carte, had arranged for the Savoy Hotel kitchen to make a cake to mark the occasion and Peter was asked to transport the cake, along with her secretary, Albert Truelove. He recalls that he and Albert had some difficulty getting the large celebration cake, on its silver tray, into the boot of his car without damage. He had a film taken that day of Bridget and John Reed walking across the Grimsdyke croquet lawn. Peter was passionate about the D'Oyly Carte and treasured his association with the company. He may have been privileged to be an insider, but he was, nonetheless, a true fan.

Another fan of the D'Oyly Carte who learned to love Gilbert and Sullivan at the feet of his father was Robin Wilson, son of Lord Wilson of Rievaulx, the former Prime Minister who served two terms in office in the 1970s. As Sir Harold Wilson, he was a lifelong G&S fan and became a trustee of the D'Oyly Carte Opera Trust in 1975. Robin, however, took a different path and enjoyed an illustrious career as a professor of mathematics, having been Head of the Pure Mathematics Department of the Open University and Dean of the Faculty amongst other distinguished positions, writing numerous books on the subject. In 1984, he somehow found time to collaborate with Frederic Lloyd, who had been the D'Oyly Carte's General Manager, on a pictorial history of the company, *Gilbert and Sullivan: The Official D'Oyly Carte Picture History*. He was always grateful that his father had influence within the D'Oyly Carte, enabling him to get tickets for special performances and invitations to formal company occasions. Robin and his father pursued extremely successful, if very different careers, but their mutual love of Gilbert and Sullivan was always there.

Some D'Oyly Carte fans successfully auditioned for the company, thereby fulfilling a long-held dream. Amongst them were principals, Cynthia Morey and Pauline Wales, both of whom had performed with amateur G&S societies as youngsters and wanted nothing more than to join the company they so admired. Cynthia bailed out of her last year at the Royal College of Music in 1951 when the chance came to go to a D'Oyly Carte audition, after which she was accepted into the company. Pauline, however, had to be patient and wait until she was considered mature enough to join. In an early audition when she was a teenager, she was told to 'come back when you're older'. Thankfully, she did, joining the chorus in 1959 and becoming a much-loved principal mezzo-soprano for ten years from 1965. Somewhat later in 1977, chorus bass, Bryan Secombe followed in the same way as Pauline, being utterly thrilled when finally told he was a suitable age to join. From boyhood, James Conroy-Ward had always wanted to be in the D'Oyly Carte Opera Company, having grown up watching the company at the Manchester Opera House. However, his route to his dream job was rather unusual. Having studied singing at the Royal Northern College of Music and the London Opera Centre, he joined the Royal Opera, spending several seasons as a chorister and small-part player at Covent Garden. And then he heard a whisper that the D'Oyly Carte was looking for an understudy to John Reed and he was off like a shot to audition. Chorus baritone and understudy, Richard Mitchell was another who had loved the company from childhood, as he explains.

'My mother, who was widowed when I was only three years old, joined the St. John's Ambulance Brigade and sometimes had to staff the Theatre Royal in Norwich in that capacity. This gave her a free ticket, which she sometimes passed on to me. On one occasion in 1964, it was for the D'Oyly Carte's *The Gondoliers*. I wasn't at all enthusiastic and took my seat with some reluctance, then the curtain went up. That was it; I was hooked! I spent days after the performance recreating the set with paper and crayons and I persuaded Mum to buy me the records for Christmas. I never dreamt that I would, one day, sit between Ken

Sandford and John Reed as Pish-Tush doing the "Cheap and Chippy Chopper" trio in *The Mikado*. Or that I would end up staying in the same very dodgy guest house in Bournemouth as my hero, John Reed!' When I asked Richard if he had any stories about the company fans, he told me this:

'Old John Hansaker (he of the single tooth) was a stalwart fan at Sadler's Wells and was always promising to reveal to us the "deliberate mistake" in the overture to *Ruddigore*. Unfortunately, he snuffed it and went to the family vault with the secret!' There were certainly some interesting characters outside theatres and Jennifer Toye, a principal soprano who was with the company from 1954 to 1965, remembers an amusing encounter between the irascible James Walker, who was Associate Musical Director at the time, and a tramp.

'We were coming out of the Manchester Opera House after the show and a vagrant was sitting on the pavement, giving a loud and unmusical rendition of "I'll Take You Home Again Kathleen". Jimmy passed by him and snapped, "You're flat!", which was rather wasted on him!' D'Oyly Carte fan or not, his audition was unsuccessful.

For all the fascinating characters who supported and followed the D'Oyly Carte around Britain, there were probably even more devoted fans of the company in North America. Sometimes having to wait many years between tours to see the company in the flesh, they were equally as enthusiastic as their trans-Atlantic counterparts. Crowds outside theatres seeking autographs and a brief word with the stars was the norm, with the performers receiving fan mail and numerous offers of hospitality. Occasionally, wealthy admirers of the company threw extravagant parties for the cast and principal soprano, Susan Jackson, remembers one in particular.

'In 1968, we were enjoying the fabulous season at the Central City Opera House in Colorado. There was hospitality galore, but the party thrown by Ellie Weckbauer was something else. The company was driven by bus from Central City, high up in the Rocky Mountains, down to Ellie's mansion in Denver. We had the freedom of the gardens and swimming pool, where we were plied with food and drinks. But the only sign of our hostess was a glimpse of her at an upstairs window, where she watched us enjoying ourselves. Later in the day, however, she made a dramatic entrance, dressed as Katisha, in a rickshaw pulled by her staff, who were also in Japanese costumes. She was obviously a great admirer of the D'Oyly Carte and it was all a bit mad, but great fun.'

Young or old, eccentric or nondescript, Stage Door perennials or anonymous audience members, the fans of the D'Oyly Carte were, from its earliest times, united in their passion for the famous company. Without their loyal support, would theatres on both sides of the Atlantic have been able to welcome professional productions of Gilbert and Sullivan for a hundred and seven years? Probably not. Sometimes irritating and demanding, sometimes delightfully amusing, many of them kind and bringers of friendship, the fans were an outside influence on the life of the company that was inescapable. If the closure in 1982 was hard to bear for performers and staff, it was much more so for the fans so devoted to the D'Oyly Carte, whose lives would never be the same again. Right at the end, only a small fraction of them were able to witness the final performance to represent their predecessors in bidding an emotional farewell. There were tears everywhere. The words of Clive Harré perfectly capture the intensity of that dreadful night.

'After The Last Night performance came the sad job of saying goodbye to the friends and colleagues with whom I had spent the last three years on tour. Emotions were high. With my wife by my side, we walked hand-in-hand through the Stage Door of London's Adelphi Theatre, but neither of us was prepared for what greeted us. Hundreds of fans stood cheering and I signed a few programmes as we pushed our way through the crowd. I remember walking down to the Embankment to get the car, but half way there I started to sob uncontrollably and I sobbed all the way home. I have never experienced such emotional exhaustion as on that night, the 27th of February, 1982.' Clive was not alone.

CHAPTER FIVE

HOW VERY AWKWARD

Perhaps one of the more obvious pressures that made D'Oyly Carte life even more difficult than usual occurred when colleagues didn't like each other, or had a falling out. Not something that happened very often, there are, nonetheless, many instances of company members having to work closely together when they would rather have not. Whatever the reasons for crossing swords with, or annoying a fellow performer, professionalism was needed to ensure audiences were oblivious to such antagonisms. However cleverly differences were covered up during performances, it was not ideal to the cause of acting if the characters were barely able to look each other in the eye to play scenes with sincerity and conviction. It is hard to imagine how those at loggerheads managed to work together at all, but they had no option but to bury the hatchet once on the stage. So how did they do it? The easy answer is to say that it was not people with a personal issue facing each other in a scene, but the characters they were playing. But was it really that simple?

In 1957, Kenneth Sandford joined the D'Oyly Carte as the new incumbent of the 'Pooh-Bah' bass-baritone roles. Playing opposite him in many of the shows would be Peter Pratt, the well-established 'patter man' and company's leading comedian. Two very different personalities, it did not take long for them to take a dislike to each other. On the surface, they were pleasant enough together, but when they had to share a dressing room, they had very little in common and conversation was never more than polite. For the newcomer, it was a tough start, but it would be another two years before Peter left the company to be replaced by the effervescent John Reed. In the meantime, Ken got on with learning the craft of performing Gilbert and Sullivan alongside a colleague who didn't like him. As 'Pooh-Bah', Ken certainly did not find it difficult to be patronising to 'Ko-Ko' when they played *Mikado*, or beseech 'Sir Ruthven' to mend his ways in the second act of *Ruddigore* but, easiest of all, was the scene in Act Two of *Patience*, when 'Grosvenor' and 'Bunthorne' had to be unpleasant to each other.

The culture shock Ken felt on joining the D'Oyly Carte was due to his down-to-earth nature and his previous jobs, which included a long run of *Carousel* in the West End, two stints of revue in Glasgow, a season of *Paint Your Wagon* and a show with the manic Crazy Gang at London's Victoria Palace Theatre. It was no wonder he found the transition to the polite gentility of the D'Oyly Carte so challenging after playing alongside so many larger-than-life theatrical personalities. Having to work closely with Peter Pratt's wife, Joyce Wright, so often his love interest as 'Phoebe' in *Yeomen* and 'Mad Margaret' in *Ruddigore*, gave him problems from the start. Her insistence that he address her as 'Miss Wright' at all times tried him sorely and he found it difficult to act their scenes as he would have liked. Her departure from the company in 1962 brought the welcome promotion from the chorus of Peggy Ann Jones, with whom Ken soon forged a happy and less-restricted working relationship. Peter and Joyce were typical old-school D'Oyly Carters, where strict etiquette and formality were the norm, so it was hardly surprising the three of them did not get along, but is to be hoped that Ken never knew about the wicked impersonation of him which Peter was known to do behind his back.

Sometimes, disagreements and arguments between colleagues were of a fleeting nature, the inevitable result of working at close quarters, or dressing room tittle-tattle getting out of hand. In any cheek-byjowel working environment, petty quarrels and irritations can lead to colleagues falling out. The D'Oyly Carte was a perfect example of such a workplace. Usually, differences were quickly settled, although Cynthia Morey remembers a mysterious upset which took a little longer to resolve.

'One evening – probably somewhere on tour – I went in at the Stage Door for a performance of *Mikado* and passed Neville Griffiths, my Nanki-Poo, who was standing there. "Hello, Neville," I said, but he simply looked right through me. I thought he was just preoccupied, or maybe worried about something and gave it no more thought, until our scene in Act One which preceded the "Kissing Duet".

'"Yum-Yum, at last we are alone,"' he said, addressing a spot on the scenery just above my left shoulder. I was tempted to turn round to see what it was, but refrained. This went on throughout the scene, and believe me, it's not easy to play a love scene and sing a duet involving kissing with no eye contact. How had I offended him? I couldn't imagine what I might, unwittingly, have done. I tried to tackle him about it, but he refused to say anything. This strange behaviour went on for several performances then, suddenly, all was sweetness and light. I'll never know what it was all about, but what I do know is that any grievances or unpleasantness between actors must be left in the wings. I've played intimate scenes with people I can't stand, but no-one would have known. There were some principals I wasn't keen on, but that's natural in a big company. Nothing affected our performances. After all, that's our job; it's what we're paid for.'

In fairness to Neville, he and Cynthia normally enjoyed an excellent working relationship, but she agreed to relate this story in order to demonstrate how awkward such a situation could be, when even a seasoned principal sometimes lost the professional plot. Her sentiments are echoed by Peggy Ann Jones, who prided herself on trying to be professional at all times, choosing not to get too close to colleagues if she thought she might not get on with them. To quote her, 'I had to feel that I had earned my wage packet.' She cites the exemplary attitude of Ann Hood and her husband, David Palmer, whose marriage broke down in the mid-1960s. As principal soprano and tenor, they worked opposite one another in romantic scenes in several of the shows and Peggy remembers the members of the company being worried about how to deal with such a difficult situation, both on and off the stage. Ann and David, however, put everyone at ease by working together as if nothing had changed between them, the ultimate in professionalism when their personal life was falling apart. How painful and difficult that must have been.

Such serious problems were uncommon in D'Oyly Carte life, most contentious issues being rather more trivial. In 1973, Maggie Bourgein's second season with the company saw an influx of gay men into the chorus. She recalls the straight men being rather miffed that she and many of the other chorus ladies chose to spend time in their convivial company rather than hang out with the heterosexual men. As she points out, 'It was not a straight versus gay issue, the gay guys were just more fun.' One might imagine problems arising from this in the men's chorus dressing room but, in general, there was a pragmatic 'live and let live attitude' towards sexuality.

In the ladies' chorus room of the 1970s there was little tolerance of those who did not conform to the expected D'Oyly Carte standards of behaviour. It was ruled by a small group of senior choristers known as 'The Royal Family' and anyone who deviated from what its members considered to be appropriate behaviour was swiftly tackled. Beti Lloyd-Jones, a chorister and contralto understudy for nearly a quarter of a century, could seem very intimidating to any newcomer, but her bark was worse than her bite. Always quick to bring people into line if she felt they were out of order, she was, nonetheless, always the first to help anyone who had a problem. I recall my first performance of *Pirates*. Young and inexperienced, I felt a sharp jab in my ribs during the first act. 'Pull your shoulders up!' Beti hissed into my ear. Scared witless, I immediately obeyed and was later told that my posture was terrible. Thanks to Beti, I grew an inch during my first season with the company as I learned to stand up straight and acquire proper theatrical deportment. The fact that it was a chorus member who, quite literally, straightened me out, did not reflect well on the Director of Productions, who obviously had not noticed that I was round-shouldered. However unapproachable and scary the The Royal Family seemed, the other chorus ladies were used to the hierarchy and stuck to their own friends unless, of course, they were invited to join the upper echelons of the chorus room, a reflection of the respect in which they were held.

To a certain extent, this culture of ruling by fear was something that newcomers to the ladies' chorus had to endure and overcome if they were to be happy in the dressing room environment, but one chorus tenor told me that the influence of The Royal Family was not confined to the women.

'From the time I joined in 1971, some of The Royal Family clearly took a dislike to me and seemed to be permanently on my back. I have no idea why this was, but it continued until the company closed in 1982 and it was not very pleasant having to work with them.'

Perhaps such behaviour makes mockery of the fabled D'Oyly Carte family but, in truth, for most of the time everyone rubbed along very well. Even the closest of families has its moments of conflict. But one young lady, who joined the chorus ranks in 1973, possessed the ability to drive everyone up the wall with her inability to conform to necessary standards of professionalism. Young and talented, she simply did not get the idea that drinking at work was completely unacceptable. After a performance in the pub yes, but not before, or during, a show. With the exception of a small sherry in the ladies' chorus room at Christmas time or, occasionally, between a matinee and evening performance, alcohol for the girls was not on the agenda. Always last out of the dressing room to go to the stage, the lady in question would put a cover over her mug containing red wine and continue drinking it on her return, assuming that no-one would notice what she was doing. Of course everyone did, but even had we not suspected a thing, the lobbing of the empty bottle into the waste bin on her way out at the end of the evening was something of a giveaway.

With her drinking habits causing consternation amongst the performers, it might be supposed that it was up to the management to take action but, as far as is known, nothing was ever said. It was rumoured that her father was a friend of someone in a senior company position, but this was purely speculation. Even more annoying to her female colleagues was her refusal to follow the rules on the wearing of a fringe when on the stage, which was forbidden. In *Ruddigore*, the bridesmaids wore ringlets pinned to their own hair, with front hair tucked under a bonnet, but the defiant young lady invariably got away with wearing a fringe down over her eyes, although frequently reminded by her colleagues not to do it. Now this may have affected her vision, but it is more likely that the demon drink caused her to once take a wrong turning during the second act number, "Happily Coupled are We", when two straight lines of bridesmaids and fisherwomen dancing at the back of the stage were unexpectedly bisected by a solitary figure sporting a straggling fringe heading for the front of the stage. Eventually ending up next to the chief bridesmaid, 'Zorah', played by Anne Egglestone, who promptly told her to 'bugger off', she danced her way back upstage and elbowed her way back into line. The astonished looks on the faces of her colleagues can be imagined but, luckily, this bizarre behaviour did not seem to distract 'Richard Dauntless' and 'Rose Maybud', played by Ralph Mason and Julia Goss. Whilst such stories are amusing, they demonstrate how maverick behaviour could cause annoyance and friction in the ordered world of the D'Oyly Carte. That one person seemed to get away with blue murder was infuriating, but it must be stressed that such things rarely happened.

I believe it fair to say that there was more of a drinking culture amongst the D'Oyly Carte's men than its ladies. If there was a backstage bar in the theatre, such as the Grand Theatre in Leeds, it was usual for some of the chorus men to enjoy a pint during a lengthy break, for example, in the second act of *Patience*, which did not require them until the finale. They kept an ear on the tannoy relaying the show so as not to be late for their next entrance, although it was not unknown for them to hear the singing of the depleted chorus from the comfort of a beer glass. In general, most of the men behaved sensibly, but Peggy Ann Jones absolutely refused to tell me the name of the chorister whom she remembers regularly needing fellow-peers either side of him in *Iolanthe* to keep him upright! In the latter days of the company, some of the men were known to keep a bottle of whisky in their dressing room. Whether this was due to specific personal problems, or dealing with life's pressures in general, it is hard to say, but it was not an ideal situation. No performer can give of their best to an audience expecting the highest professional standards when reliant on a drink to get them through a performance. Spare a thought, too, for the ladies who had to partner them in a show. There was nothing more unpleasant than having to work at close quarters with someone reeking of booze. It must, however, be stressed that most D'Oyly Carters took their job very seriously and did not drink whilst at work.

Unpleasant personal habits inflicted on colleagues were always unwelcome, so in the hot, oppressive atmosphere of a theatre, good hygiene was absolutely essential, particularly given that D'Oyly Carte costumes were cleaned only once a year. Hard to believe maybe, but a company touring year-round on a tight budget had neither the time to get costumes dry-cleaned, nor the luxury of a second set for each opera. Even had this been the case, transporting double the number of costumes would have been impractical. It was, therefore, understandable that bad breath, body odour, or lack of cleanliness was intolerable. The stink of sweat in the dressing room was bad enough, but it was horrible to have to work closely with a partner who did not smell good. But who had the responsibility of approaching an offender? It is never the easiest subject to bring to the attention of someone in need of a relationship with a bar of soap, so how was this awkward situation managed? The obvious answer, one might imagine, would be for the Wardrobe Mistress to have a quiet word with anyone falling short in the cleanliness department. Was it down to one colleague having the courage to tell another that they had a problem? Most people would baulk at the idea of approaching such a delicate matter and D'Oyly Carters tended to pass the buck to someone else. In the 1960s, the ladies of the chorus came up with the perfect fall-guy, as Peter Riley relates.

'I think perhaps one of the most difficult things I had to do as a young Stage Manager was after the ladies' chorus had abandoned all realistic attempts to indicate to a new chorister that a body odour problem was prominent. The dropping of gentle hints such as antiperspirants, talcum powder and fragrances being left on the person's make-up place proving futile, it fell to me, following several deputations from a body of the ladies' chorus, to intervene and exercise my modest, but well-known, charms upon the young maiden in question. It was a desperate, last-ditch attempt to ban the furious and fragrant ladies of the chorus from setting upon and de-robing the lady with the hygiene problem.'

Peter's account may be somewhat tongue-in-cheek, but he would argue that the poor Stage Manager always got the dirty jobs. The theatre has never been the cleanest of working environments, but having to wear heavy costumes in very hot weather, it was hardly surprising that sweating was a constant problem. In the days before air-conditioned dressing rooms, working in oppressively hot conditions was the norm; you got used to it. I particularly remember the Boston season during the 1976 tour of North America. It was high summer and the temperature outside the theatre was in the nineties, so it was well over one hundred degrees in the dressing rooms, where opening windows provided no relief. We were performing *The Mikado*, the costumes for which were exceptionally heavy. Once on the stage, the extra heat of the stage lighting made it almost unbearable and during one performance I was close to fainting. That was for a chorister, so how much more difficult for the principals with all the responsibility of their roles? There was nowhere to hide from the heat for them; sweltering in ridiculously hot temperatures, they had to sing, act and dance as well as if they were in cool, comfortable conditions. It was tough. We pitied, in particular, Kenneth Sandford as 'Pooh-Bah', swathed in layers of body-bulking padding underneath his enormous costume. The glamour of the theatre? Not at such times.

Much has been said about the camaraderie that traditionally existed within the company, but one man, who joined the chorus in the mid-1970s, soon became aware a culture of systematic bullying in the dressing room. He recalls two or three perpetrators who could make life very unpleasant for anyone they picked out as targets for their venom. During a conversation I had with him, it became apparent that he had been on the receiving end of such treatment for the whole of the time he was with the D'Oyly Carte. He recalls it starting soon after he joined, following a compliment paid to him by a member of the management which was overheard by one of the bullies. Thereafter, snide remarks and taunting became the norm and it was evident to me that talking about this abuse brought back to him the painful memories buried for over three decades, along with deep regret for passively accepting that such treatment had to be silently endured rather than tackled head on. Neither he, nor any of his colleagues did anything about it. How stressful that must have been.

I admit to being shocked by this revelation, having never witnessed such behaviour in the ladies' chorus room, or ever having heard whispers about bullying amongst the men. But, on reflection, I can believe it. In any close-knit working group there will be the occasional instance of someone proving to be unpopular with work-mates and the D'Oyly Carte was no exception. I do remember one such person being subjected to sniggering and whispered comments from a small section of the male chorus whenever he went on for a part, particularly so if he made a mistake. Although inaudible to the audience, such cruel remarks were clearly heard by those on the stage and obviously designed to undermine the confidence of the unfortunate performer. And yes, we all heard it, but did nothing about it. Was this because we thought the victim deserved it? Possibly so, which did not reflect well on any of us. Yet, I cannot recall such unkind treatment being stopped by the management, most likely, it must be supposed, because they were unaware that it was happening. Given that the company prided itself on its family atmosphere, it is uncomfortable to be reminded of the darker side of D'Oyly Carte life. Distance lends enchantment and it is easier to remember the fun times rather than the less-savoury events which sullied the clean-cut image of the company.

In the above instances of bullying, the victims new full well the identity of those who made their lives a misery, but this was not always the case. Susan Jackson, a principal soprano from 1967 to 1969, never felt truly at home within the company and always had the feeling that, as she told me, 'someone had it in for her'. Whether it was a fellow performer, or a member of the management, she had no idea, but it came as no real surprise when told by the company's General Manager, Frederic Lloyd, that her contract was not being renewed.

'I told him that if that was the way he felt I would leave immediately, but was told in no uncertain terms that I would see out my contract.' To this day, she has no idea why she felt she was being targeted, but the conviction that there was subtle pressure to get her out is as strong today, some fifty years later, as it was then.

Having spent the first two seasons of his D'Oyly Carte career struggling to get along with Peter Pratt, Kenneth Sandford welcomed the promotion of John Reed to principal comedian in 1959. The two men liked each other, happily sharing their time together in the dressing room and on the stage, where they forged a dynamic working relationship which was not lost on audiences. They became the dream team, bringing a mutual understanding and magic to their scenes. Some sixteen years later, around the time of the company's centenary celebrations, Ken noticed an unexpected cooling in John's attitude towards him which left him mystified. The two men had not quarrelled and Ken had no idea as to why John seemed to have distanced himself. Their work, of course, did not suffer, but there was a distinct chill in the dressing room. This situation remained until John left the D'Oyly Carte in 1979.

Whether or not Ken ever tried to put matters right between them is not certain, but it is probably unlikely. Although hurt by John's attitude towards him after so many years of friendship, he was the sort of man to shrug his shoulders and let John get on with it. However, he had a theory as to why John had turned against him. As part of the D'Oyly Carte centenary celebrations in 1975, a new production of *Utopia Limited* was planned. Casting, according to Peter Riley, the Technical Director at the time, was in the hands of the Stage Director and Musical Director in consultation with Bridget D'Oyly Carte and General Manager, Frederic Lloyd. John was given the part of 'Scaphio' opposite John Ayldon's 'Phantis'. This left Ken to play 'King Paramount', a hugely challenging role which he embraced with gusto. Although reviews of the revival were, generally, lukewarm, Ken was universally praised for his tour-de-force performance, bringing all his experience in comedy acting and singing to the demanding part. Ken told me that he thought that John regretted having the smaller part which left him out of the limelight. Jealousy? Perhaps, but their relationship further dipped in 1979, when Ken took a dim view of the demands John made of the Savoy Hill management if he was to remain with the company after the tour of Australia and New Zealand, which Ken saw as little short of blackmail. But not long before his death, John told a mutual friend that he had never worked with anyone as good as Ken Sandford and that he couldn't remember why they had fallen out. Sad, nonetheless, that two giants of the D'Oyly Carte should end their illustrious working relationship on such a sour note. Peter Riley perfectly sums up the situation:

'With regard to the friendship between John Reed and Ken Sandford, I always felt it was somewhat tenuous on John's side. It was a great disappointment to me that it ended the way it did in a genuine fall out after two such superb artistes had worked so closely together for so many years. I remember, in Adelaide, getting them together and insisting that they shake hands after their final performance together. I thought how sad it was that it had come to this.'

It was not always clashes between performers that could cause stress; it was not uncommon for members of the production staff to create difficult situations. Previously, I detailed the problems with Leonard Osborn encountered by several principals who felt they were being undermined by the former principal tenor appointed as Director of Productions in 1977. It is not an exaggeration to say that his high-handed manner irritated everyone. Michael Buchan, understudy to John Ayldon, once had to deputise as 'Arac' in *Princess Ida*. Going on as a cover in one of the less-frequently performed operas invariably meant appearing with very little rehearsal and Mike had the added pressure of having to get into a full suit of armour, complete with heavy longsword. Whilst practising strapping on the numerous elements of the armour with his dresser, Osborn repeatedly made calls over the tannoy for Mike to be given notes. Angered by the director's impatience, Mike finally clanked onto the stage and gave Mr Osborn a piece of his mind. Hardly ideal preparation for a nerve-racking performance, which Mike felt should have been recognised.

My own experience of difficulty with a Stage Director involved Michael Heyland, whom I always felt disliked me, although I had no idea why this should be. During rehearsals for his new production of *Utopia Limited* for the centenary season, the 'presentation scene' early in the second act saw the chorus ladies make individual entrances to the court in the manner of debutantes. I was instructed by Mr Heyland to trip up, the only lady told to do this. To me, it seemed ridiculous, because the audience would have no way of knowing as to whether this was intentional or accidental. I had a suspicion that it was to make me look silly, so I followed this direction throughout the rehearsal period, but glided elegantly on for opening night without the stumble. I think it likely my last-minute decision was down to the fact that my parents had travelled down to London for the performance and the thought of embarrassing them was too much to bear. Interestingly, Mr Heyland said nothing about my refusal to do as asked, so I was trip-free for the rest of the run.

Whether or not company members got on with each other, the demands of D'Oyly Carte life on its performers in having to give eight shows a week are easy enough to imagine. As a business run without outside financial support, the revenue from so many performances was critical to the company's survival. This demanding schedule, which saw most of the principals on the stage four or five times a week, with the principal comedian, or 'patter man', and leading contralto usually appearing six times a week, was unique in the world of opera. Most opera singers would quail at the thought of doing more than two or three performances a week, the strain on their voices unimaginable, but so it was for D'Oyly Carte stars. Vocal stamina was of paramount importance, along with the ability to maintain a high quality of performance during every week of year-round touring. With time to rest and recover in short supply, the news that the company was to make a new recording would be received by the over-worked principals with a mix of excitement and trepidation. The thrill of committing the interpretation of their roles to posterity being tempered by the worry of their voices being fresh enough to do themselves justice.

During the company's long history, the Savoy Operas were regularly recorded under the D'Oyly Carte banner, so how did the company cope with fitting recording sessions into its already full schedule? The earliest recording, *The Mikado*, made under the auspices of Rupert D'Oyly Carte in 1917, along with *The Gondoliers* in 1919, featured singers not associated with the company, so there was no clash with performances. Gradually, during the 1920s, company performers were introduced to recordings, to the delight of loyal audiences wanting to buy records featuring the stars they were accustomed to seeing at the Savoy Theatre. When the era of electrical recording began, the company started afresh with new recordings and, thereafter, periodically produced records until the late 1970s, which meant finding time to fit in studio sessions between eight performances a week.

For the chorus members, the welcome extra work presented no difficulty. However late a night they might have had, turning up to sing at a morning recording session safe in the knowledge that there was no individual responsibility was easy, as a future principal soprano, Cynthia Morey, told me:

'The only recordings I did as a chorister were *The Sorcerer*, which would have been around 1952/53 and the great one-line solo of Sacharissa in *Princess Ida* in 1954. I certainly did not feel overworked in any way; I was young and life was exciting. We recorded at the Decca studios in Broadhurst Gardens, West Hampstead and, as far as I can remember, three-hour sessions were paid at £2!'

For the principals, however, it was another matter. If they were lucky, they would not have been appearing the previous night. If they were unlucky, a Sunday session could see them having to be vocally prepared by 10am, having done two performances the previous day, as was often the case for the principal comedians and contraltos. The recording studio was a very pressurised environment and even the most seasoned performers felt the nerves of having to deliver their best work knowing that a couple of takes were all they were likely to get. Studio time was costly and scheduling was tight, so there was little opportunity to go back and perfect a number as they would have liked. Peggy Ann Jones remembers one embarrassing session when recording *The Mikado* in 1973. Playing 'Pitti-Sing', she could not understand why the technicians in the booth were looking puzzled and kept demanding another take, because they were hearing a tinny, rattling noise whenever she was singing. During the fourth attempt to get a clean recording, Peggy was doing the same broad gestures she would use on the stage, when her eye went to the clinking charm bracelet sliding up and down her wrist. Still singing, she hurriedly pulled down the sleeve of her dress and clasped her hands together, delighted to be given the thumbs up at last.

Peggy explains that by using gestures as if in a performance, she found it easy to capture her character and act through the music, although she had to be careful not to overdo it, causing her to have to take a deep breath which might be audible. She recalls Thomas Round once taking her to task on this: he was adamant that the music alone was of importance during the making of a record and that acting had to take a back seat. Ever the actress, Peggy's response? 'For me, it's impossible to separate the two. Ken Sandford was the same; no wonder they always put us together.'

Perhaps the final challenge for principals in the recording studio was the isolation of standing alone in front of a microphone with the eyes and ears of every chorus member upon them; it took a special kind of guts and talent to produce a great performance for posterity. Then, of course, was the pressure of hearing the recording they had made played back, when self-criticism kicked in, along with the worry of what other people would think of their performance. Given that they were often tired and nervous, it is remarkable that so many D'Oyly Carte stars left behind them the wonderful performances on record that are still enjoyed today.

At least a recording session gave principals the opportunity to correct any glaring mistakes, but not so during a live radio broadcast, when one shot was all they got. If the pressure felt by solo performers in the recording studio was bad enough, then how much more so knowing that hundreds of thousands of listeners were tuning in to hear a rare D'Oyly Carte performance on air? As part of the centenary season, a performance of *The Mikado*, conducted by Sir Charles Mackerras, was relayed live by the BBC from the Savoy Theatre. It is not difficult to imagine the trepidation of those standing in the wings waiting to go on and for one of the principals, the unthinkable happened, when nerves overtook experience and normally-assured technique.

I remember being in the ladies' chorus dressing room, some energy-sapping ninety steps up at the top of the building, where we were listening with interest to the start of the show, hoping that everyone did themselves proud and then looking at each other in horror when poor Colin Wright, playing 'Nanki-Poo', cracked on a top note in "A Wand'ring Minstrel I". How we felt for him having to carry on as if nothing had happened. Despite being an experienced principal, the pressure of the occasion must have caused such an unusual misjudgement. It was the sort of unfortunate mishap that can haunt a performer for years. Colleagues may commiserate, but the embarrassment of such a gaffe is never completely forgotten.

But there were other banana skins to be avoided when taking part in a live broadcast, like those occasioned by having to wear a radio microphone. D'Oyly Carte performers were schooled in the old ways of voice projection, so the unfamiliar use of a mic was not unknown to cause problems for them, particularly if the sound engineer accidentally forgot to close a soloist's individual channel. Pity the conscientious singer doing vocal exercises backstage discovering that their noisy arpeggios had, for a brief moment, been shared with audience and listeners. Worse still for the poor soul who paid a visit to the loo during a live performance! Kenneth Sandford, however, who should have known better, could hardly blame the sound man when he completely forgot his live microphone whilst dancing with Lorraine

Daniels during the broadcast of a concert, treating the listeners to his unscripted dialogue, 'Round you go, love.'

While the D'Oyly Carte singers enjoyed the financial benefits of recording contracts, the members of the company's orchestra were not so fortunate, as it was usual for a big name orchestra, such as the Royal Philharmonic, to be used instead of the regular musicians in the pit who experienced the same hardships of life on tour as the performers on the stage above them. Unsung heroes who seldom received recognition for their part in a successful performance, they were used to playing second fiddle to the singers. Although taking part in the same creative process, the two factions of performers tended to lead separate artistic lives. Clarinettist, Howard Rogerson gives us an insight into the stresses and hardships of life in the D'Oyly Carte orchestra in which he performed for four years from 1971.

'I joined the Musicians' Union whilst still an undergraduate at the Royal Manchester College of Music. Two years later, I was asked to deputise with the famous D'Oyly Carte Opera Company during its Manchester season of 1971 and was subsequently offered three weeks with the company for its seasons in Torquay and Taunton. This led to me being invited to go on the Autumn tour of Scotland, not only as second clarinet, but also as repetiteur, rehearsing the singers. I declined the offer of repetiteur and was informed that, after this vacancy had been advertised, if a clarinettist was engaged for the post, then I would not be! By good fortune, a violinist was given the job, so I was engaged as second clarinet. Two weeks into the tour, the first clarinettist decided to leave and, after an audition, I was offered the first position, which allowed me to perform in the Sadler's Wells Christmas season. In those days, the touring players were engaged for London, when the orchestral numbers were augmented, but the strings moved to back desks, with the wind and brass principals dropping down to second players, whilst the second players were put out of work. Fortunately, with the help of the Musicians' Union and the Association of British Orchestras, we managed to change this arrangement for the following 1972 season.'

The idea that some of the instrumentalists were considered by the D'Oyly Carte management to be proficient for provincial performances, but not for London performances must have been rather insulting both to them and provincial audiences, but with work always in short supply, players took what they could get. But being in-and-out of work was just one of the problems for hard-working musicians. Conditions in theatres were often bordering on unpleasant and payment was barely adequate, as Howard remembers only too well.

'Pits were small and dirty for the twenty-four-piece touring orchestra, and changing facilities usually comprised of one small band room for both sexes. There were no rehearsals, just straight in to performances, so sight-reading had to be excellent, as had spatial awareness of the music and those around you. When I started, my weekly pay as a principal player was £22, with £7 subsistence allowance, plus travel money equivalent to a second-class rail fare. One could never find digs for £7 a week, it was always more. Then there was the cost of meals and rent for home base accommodation. Payment was made every Friday, when we had to queue up outside the touring manager's office, which was often just a small dressing room. Gerry Kripps, the percussionist, would always stand and wait for a donation to the Musicians' Union Benevolent Fund. However, when we were in London, we were paid by an orchestral management company and received a minimum of £40 a week, but with no subsistence allowance.

'Every new theatre meant we had to have a three-hour seating rehearsal, for which we were not paid, and this often included some of the singers wanting to re-run an aria, or were covering roles. Our contracts were for eight performances a week, so this was extra work. Often after these seating rehearsals, letters from audience members would be read out, usually making adverse comments about the behaviour of the orchestra, or their dress – and even "Why do they have to make such a noise before the performance?" All these years on, I am still in touch with my bassoonist friend, David Catchpole, who was the librarian, and also one of the oboists.'

It is true to say that although singers and orchestra members were friendly enough, they tended to be part of separate entities and their paths seldom crossed. There were, naturally, exceptions to this, as Valerie Masterson would surely agree, when she took a shine to Andrew March, a flautist in the orchestra, who was to become her husband. There were other instances of personal relationships developing between pit and stage, but it did not often happen. Friendships were occasionally forged on tour but, by and large, singers and musicians lived separate lives. Howard Rogerson looked forward to the rare social occasions which brought everyone together.

'Whilst on Scottish tours, the company members would be invited to after-show events, or just allowed to use clubs, such as the English-Speaking Club in Aberdeen, the Musicians' Club in Glasgow and a Gentlemen's Club in Edinburgh. I remember the Lord Mayor of Manchester inviting everyone to dine with him in the Banqueting Rooms of the magnificent Waterhouse Town Hall. It was a grand occasion. Such events helped me to get to know the other company members, including the singers, otherwise we would only see them on the stage, or pass them on the stairs and in corridors. In 1975, Dame Bridget D'Oyly Carte invited everyone to dinner at the Savoy Hotel to celebrate the company's centenary. Sadly, as we had to pay for ourselves, I declined as it was so expensive.'

Howard's final comment says much about the D'Oyly Carte. That the figurehead of such a famous company could not treat all of her employees to dinner on the occasion of its centenary seems penny-pinching to say the least. But was there more to it than that? According to Peter Riley, who was the company's Technical Director at the time, quite possibly.

'I rather imagine that Dame Bridget's secretary, Albert Truelove, had more than quite a lot to do with it. He never liked spending money and didn't agree with enlarging the orchestra for London seasons because of the cost. It was natural that all the playing company were invited, plus the permanent staff, but it's likely that, as only half of the orchestra was used in London, he would suggest that they could attend the dinner, but would have to pay. I know that Dame Bridget would have entrusted the arrangements to Albert, but she would have been horrified to learn that anyone invited to the centenary dinner at the Savoy was expected to pay for a celebration supper.'

Money was always an issue for the D'Oyly Carte and it was never in a position to pay its workers well. Without public funding, the company's operation relied on Box Office receipts for its income. However, a job with the D'Oyly Carte was always highly prized, because it offered year-round security of employment, something few other companies could match. Low pay brought many pressures, particularly to those with a family to support. The cost of touring accommodation, travel expenses, household rent, mortgages and child support caused many a financial juggling act as performers and staff struggled to make ends meet.

Managing on a low salary was much easier for the better-paid principals, or choristers who were single, particularly if their home base was with parents. My starting pay in 1972 was £22 per week, which, on the surface of it, was a good wage packet in those days. But factor in the cost of accommodation and running a car and there was very little left over. Car owners were paid the equivalent of a single rail ticket to help with travelling, but tax, insurance and maintenance ate into weekly pay. It was lucky that I still lived in the family home and I certainly found the introduction of a small touring allowance, two years after I joined the company, was a big help, but it was still a tight budget. However, for company members who were married, or had their own home, it was another matter.

There were many similarities between Kenneth Sandford and Jon Ellison. Both served the D'Oyly Carte for over twenty years; both were married (Jon to former company member, Joy Mornay); both owned their own homes and both had two children. However, as a senior principal, Ken earned far more than Jon, a chorister who played small roles. Their financial commitments were not dissimilar, but the difference was that Ken, on his bigger salary, was able to give his son and daughter a private education. Both Gordon 'Mike' Mackenzie and Michael Rayner had large families, with nine children between them, so how either of them managed to support their numerous offspring on their D'Oyly Carte pay is something of a mystery. Gordon, who served several stints as a chorus tenor from 1954 before graduating to touring management in 1969, lived in Greenock, so getting back to Scotland to see his family happened very infrequently. In fact, there was a good-natured joke within the company that he had four kids, but had only been home three times!

Throughout the company's long history there were very few instances of married women who left their husbands at home whist they went on long tours, but one such example was Pamela Baxter, a chorus mezzo-soprano for several years until the company closed. Her marriage was strong and her husband seemed to happily accept that she chose to work away from home for so much of every year. Between them, they made a good living. In truth, it was much easier for the D'Oyly Carte's single employees to cope with the financial stresses of touring. It was a much less-difficult life with no family responsibility and the chance to make the most of any spare cash. Chorus baritone, Thomas Scholey, loved nothing more than fine dining and indulged his passion whenever he could. Yet the married men within the company somehow managed to survive the financial hardship of looking after a family on a similar wage to Thomas, some doing so for many years. I like to think this says something about the satisfaction of working for such a unique organisation. Others may disagree.

As if the rigours of performing up to eight shows every week for eleven months were not hard enough, it is clear that there were numerous other causes of stress to be managed alongside normal contractual obligations. From dressing room disagreements, sweaty colleagues, personality clashes, coping with illness, poor pay and working conditions, to the perils of the microphone, there was seldom a dull moment for hard-pressed D'Oyly Carters. However did we do it?

CHAPTER SIX

WHATEVER NEXT?

It is clear that the D'Oyly Carte was not a career choice for the faint of heart. If its performers were able to deal with the pressures and hardships of life on tour, the rewards could far outweigh the disadvantages. Security of employment; the chance to perform in great theatres; the potential for career advancement; the opportunity of overseas travel and the forging of life-long friendships awaited those hardy enough to withstand the rigours of life permanently on the move. There were some for whom the D'Oyly Carte lifestyle became a comfortable habit, seeing them remain with the company for a quarter of a century or more. Others soon discovered that being an itinerant thespian was not for them and a year on the road was enough. During the one hundred and seven year history of the company, almost three thousand performers graced the D'Oyly Carte stage and for all of them, whatever the reason, the time came when they left to begin another life and career. The different paths they took are fascinating, from the obvious progression into other theatre work, to the most unlikely choice of occupation for an ex-theatrical. Exploring just a few post-

D'Oyly Carte careers demonstrates the variety of employment choices that were made. Some are surprising.

John Dennison auditioned for the D'Oyly Carte Opera Company whilst the company was on tour in North America. British by birth, he had moved to America as a young man to pursue a career as a professional opera singer, but he had always loved Gilbert and Sullivan and the lure of a job with the D'Oyly Carte was too much to resist. Accepted into the chorus, he sailed to England and began his time with the company in May 1956. He loved his new life, made many friends and looked forward to remaining in Britain, but family commitments meant he would leave after just fifteen months. In July of 1957, he left the company and returned to America. Although he found work as a singer, he needed other work to top up his income, so turned to his love of motor cars. This eventually led to him owning his own business in West Chester, Pennsylvania, selling, restoring and maintaining classic Rolls Royce cars.

From then on, he pursued two careers, continuing as a successful professional singer at the same time as having his head under the bonnets of luxury motors. John was well into his seventies when he retired from doing up posh cars and sold his company, but he continued to sing for his supper. Now ninety-one, he has recently appeared as 'Major-General Stanley' in *The Pirates of Penzance* and his remarkable baritone voice is still well-oiled. As for the cars he so lovingly cosseted they, too, are still running smoothly. I can confirm this, having ridden in style in the 'Roller' he sold to a friend of mine, who treasures it as a mobile gin palace.

Yvonne Sommeling was one of a number of graduates of the Birmingham School of Music to join the D'Oyly Carte over a five-year period from 1967. In 1970, she was accepted into the chorus alongside John Broad and Anne Egglestone, before Michael Rayner came in as a principal baritone a year later, followed by myself in 1972. A stunningly glamorous girl, Yvonne was never a conventional D'Oyly Carte young lady, often causing ripples in the traditionally conservative company with her provocative sense of fashion and 'who cares' attitude. She certainly caught the eye of Stage Manager, Peter Riley, the couple marrying after she left in 1972.

Following her departure from the company, she found work as a model and actress, but the breakdown of her marriage led her in a completely different direction, to South Africa in 1982. There, she met her second husband and re-discovered her love of painting. In the following years, it is no exaggeration to say that she has become one of her adopted country's greatest artists. Her passion for its wildlife and people, whom she often portrays in quirky settings, has led to her work becoming highly prized around the world. Yvonne's paintings are to be found in private collections in countries across Europe to the Middle East, New Zealand and the Far East. She has recently had an exhibition at the Moscow State Art Gallery but, perhaps, her greatest claim to fame was being commissioned to paint a portrait of Nelson Mandela, which has pride of place in the Mandela House Museum in Soweto. A photograph of Yvonne with Mr Mandela can be seen on her website. I think it right to say that she has come a long way since those days when she caused shock waves in the D'Oyly Carte by wearing miniskirts and hot pants.

Some three years after Yvonne left the company, another chorister of rebellious nature, Rosalind Griffiths, exited the D'Oyly Carte at the same time as her future husband, John Broad and, by coincidence, she, too, has become something of an artist, designing and painting greetings cards when her singing engagements permit. But, her working life in the intervening years has been varied to say the least.

'After I left the Carte, trying to find work as an opera singer proved difficult, so I got a singing teaching post at Loughborough University, where John and I were living at the time. When we moved to Somerset, I decided on a different career path and trained to be a lifeguard. It was a job I loved but, after a year, I found, much to my annoyance, that I was putting on a lot of weight, so every night after work, I took to swimming twenty lengths and working out in the gym for half an hour before heading home. It didn't make any difference, so I went to the doctor, who announced that I was expecting twins! I stayed on at work, training other lifeguards but, as my pregnancy progressed, I became absolutely enormous, struggling to keep up with my charges as I waddled around the swimming pool in their wake, so that was that.

'Some time after my sons were born, I saw an advert for a job as a kennel maid which really appealed as I love dogs and I was selected from a list of fourteen other women. Looking forward to starting, I was horrified when I arrived for my first day to find that I would be looking after cats which were being used in a trial for a new kind of pet food. I hate cats! Things got worse when, after a few days, I began to get all sorts of unpleasant symptoms and I was sacked when my bosses found out I was allergic to the furry little darlings. Thereafter, I got employment working for Pedigree pet foods, but this was just one of about thirty various jobs I had over the years. There was never a dull moment, but I kept my singing going all the time and always enjoyed any gigs I got, especially the shows I did with John.'

For all the different jobs she took on, Ros must have found the time to practise her singing, because she still has a glorious voice and is no mean actress. Still as feisty as in her younger days, she is a terrific performer. Rather wasted on pet food in my opinion.

Ros's husband, John Broad, was one of many ex-Carters who became teachers. For most, teaching singing was an obvious way to earn a living between engagements, or after they had retired from the stage. Amongst the most successful have been Gillian Knight, Valerie Masterson and Pamela Field, but there are many others who still impart their hard-earned vocal skills to aspiring singers. The company's last principal soubrette, Lorraine Daniels, teaches at several secondary schools in Essex. I guess that she accompanies her students because, as I remember, she is an excellent pianist. Amongst others to teach singing for many years are Suzanne O'Keeffe, Kevin West, Jane Robinson and Norman Wilfred Wright.

When Norman and his wife, principal contralto, Christene Palmer, left the company in 1971, both found work as freelance singers but, in 1976, they decided to move to Australia to live in Geelong, Christene's home town. Norman secured a part-time position at the Melbourne Conservatorium of Music, but this was not sufficient to make ends meet, so he worked for a life assurance company when not teaching. Deciding to cash in on their D'Oyly Carte experience, the couple mounted successful Gilbert and Sullivan concerts, working alongside their former Carte colleague, Dennis Olsen, who often stayed with them. Sadly, after four years, with three small children to support, what Norman describes as their 'big mistake' was over and they returned to England, settling in Nuneaton in Warwickshire. However, after being away for so long, Norman found it difficult to pick up work from his previous contacts, so teaching singing was an obvious course of action. He and Christene also produced shows for amateur operatic societies in the Midlands, but his teaching practice has always been their mainstay and he is still in demand.

For other teachers, academia was the preferred choice. John Broad had trained as a teacher before being inveigled into joining the D'Oyly Carte Opera Company against his better judgement. After a successful six years with the company, during which time he played and understudied many roles, but was best-known as a brilliant 'Notary' in *The Sorcerer*, 'The Lieutenant of the Tower' in *The Yeomen of the Guard* and 'The Usher' in *Trial by Jury*, John was ready to pursue his ultimate ambition to teach. His career off-stage was equally successful and he spent many years, until retirement, as Head Teacher of a secondary school in Somerset. Tenor choristers of the 1970s, Edwin Rolles and John Coe-Roper also went into school teaching on leaving the company. On the closure of the D'Oyly Carte, chorus soprano, Christine George, returned to her professional roots as a school teacher, both in Staffordshire and her native South Wales, until retiring a few years ago.

Principal baritone from an earlier era, Jeffrey Skitch came late to teaching, but went on to a successful thirty-year school career. Having studied law whilst on tour with the company, Jeffrey was not satisfied with this and, after leaving the D'Oyly Carte in 1965, he gained a degree in biological science from London University, which led to posts at the prestigious Oakham School in Rutland and Malvern College. One might think this would have been enough for him but, in 1985, his teaching career took an unexpected turn when he was appointed as principal of the Elmhurst Ballet School, alongside his American wife as vice-principal. I think it not unfair to say that this caused more than a few raised eyebrows amongst his former Carte colleagues, who found it hard to believe he had landed such a job when he had never been noted for his dancing skills on the stage. Theirs was not to reason why.

Of course, an obvious direction for most ex-D'Oyly Carters was a continuation of their careers in the theatre and, indeed, many made a good living in opera and music theatre. The success enjoyed by Valerie Masterson in the world's great opera houses has been well-documented and she is, undoubtedly, the most illustrious singer ever to emerge from the D'Oyly Carte. A true diva, she was adored by her many fans and ranked in the highest echelons of the opera world. But Valerie was not the only company member to grace the operatic stage. Principal contralto, Gillian Knight, was another to win acclaim for her performances in grand opera and Kenneth Sandford was once heard to say, after he saw her in the title role of *Carmen* at The Royal Opera House, that he was captivated by the performance of the woman he had only ever known as one of W.S. Gilbert's dreaded old ladies. Kenneth, himself, was never short of work after the closure of the company. Although never lucky enough to fulfil his ambition to appear in grand opera, he was always in demand for concerts and productions of G&S on both sides of the Atlantic. His passion for working on his vocal technique never left him and he practised every day, his voice still glorious when he passed away at the age of eighty.

A contemporary of Kenneth, Valerie and Gillian was principal bass, Donald Adams, who was hugely popular for sixteen years with D'Oyly Carte audiences in the 'Mikado roles'. On leaving the company in 1969, he concentrated for many years on *Gilbert and Sullivan For All*, the company he formed with Music Director, Norman Meadmore, and his great friend, the ever-popular principal tenor, Thomas Round. Together, they toured the world with their G&S concerts and productions of the Savoy Operas, which featured many of their former Carte colleagues. However, in 1983, Donald turned towards grand opera, making his Covent Garden debut in *Boris Godunov*. Before long, he was in demand all over the world, but was most often seen appearing with English National Opera and Welsh National Opera. Just a month before his death in 1996, he had performed in Donizetti's *Don Pasquale* and was preparing a role in Britten's *A Midsummer Night's Dream* for the Metropolitan Opera in New York. For all their many successes in opera, Valerie, Gillian and Donald always recognised the importance of the D'Oyly Carte in launching their later careers.

In a matter of ten years, soprano Vivian Tierney went from dance band singer to a successful career in grand opera via five years in the D'Oyly Carte. Joining the company as a gauche chorister with a glorious voice, she quickly fulfilled her potential and developed into an accomplished principal. After the company's final season, she went on to appear regularly with English National Opera, Opera North and

Glyndebourne. Her marriage to a Canadian and their decision to live a quiet life in Canada cut short her career, robbing the opera world of a true talent.

Just a year before Vivian joined the D'Oyly Carte in 1975, chorus tenor, Adrian Martin, left the company after three years in search of pastures new. He would have been the first to agree that his raw voice had potential, but needed work. He obviously found an excellent singing teacher because, within three years, he had made his Covent Garden debut in Richard Strauss' *Salome*. Thereafter, he appeared regularly with English National Opera and Opera North, with appearances around Europe and in Australia. I can personally attest to his transformation, having seen him as the 'Steersman' in Wagner's *The Flying Dutchman*. I was little short of astounded by his wonderful voice and the confident performance none of us would have thought possible from him whilst he was with the D'Oyly Carte.

Sadly, his burgeoning career was cut tragically short by serious illness around 1990. However, he was persuaded to return to the stage, appearing as 'Ralph Rackstraw', playing opposite Valerie Masterson, as 'Josephine' in *HMS Pinafore* at the Opera House in Buxton, as part of the International Gilbert and Sullivan Festival of 1997. I was privileged to direct that production and thoroughly enjoyed working with him, but his health never improved sufficiently for him to resume his life as a successful opera singer. He died in 2014. Such a waste of talent.

Numerous D'Oyly Carte choristers have enjoyed lengthy careers with Britain's opera companies and, indeed, Bryan Secombe and Michael Lessiter can still be seen in the Royal Opera chorus. The English National Opera chorus boasted ex-Carters aplenty. Keith Bonnington and his wife, Anne Egglestone, Derek Booth, Glyn Adams and his wife, Elizabeth Mynett and Joseph Riordan, to name but a few. In 1989, soprano, Alexandra Hann, joined the Welsh National Opera Chorus, working alongside former Carte principal tenor, Ralph Mason, and fellow-choristers, Caroline Baker and Glynis Prendergast. For some twenty years, Opera North enjoyed the services of another D'Oyly Carte principal tenor, Harold Sharples, before he completely changed direction and became an Advanced Driving Instructor.

It was not just the world of opera that sustained many a D'Oyly Carter after they left the company. Musicals proved a rich vein of employment and Andrew Lloyd-Webber's perennial favourite, *The Phantom of the Opera*, saw a steady stream of ex-D'Oyly Carte performers joining the successful show. The original cast included Barry Clark and Jill Washington in small named roles. Jill was later promoted to the leading part of 'Christine', a role she played for several lengthy seasons. She is reputed to have played the part more than any other soprano in the world. Another Carte principal soprano, Julia Goss, had a successful run in the role of 'Carlotta'. Others to appear in the show were Peggy Ann Jones, Guy Matthews and John Ayldon. Another Lloyd-Webber blockbuster, *Evita*, featured Jon Ellison, Lyndsie Holland and Julia Goss on a nationwide tour.

The list of West End musicals featuring D'Oyly Carte performers is lengthy, but it is worth noting that Cynthia Morey, a principal soprano in the 1950s, appeared in *Me and My Girl* at London's Adelphi Theatre in 1985, alongside Bruce Graham, a Carter from two decades later. As President and Vice-President, respectively, of The Gilbert and Sullivan Society, their paths still regularly cross. Having left the company in 1957, Cynthia has rarely been away from the theatre. Her list of credits over the intervening years is impressive, including twelve years with Sadler's Wells Opera Company, appearances in pantomime, revue and numerous West End musicals, the latter taking her to Europe, North America, Australia and New Zealand. Most recently, she appeared in the film, *Quartet*, directed by Dustin Hoffman. Now ninety-two years old, Cynthia is a true theatre animal, whose wealth of stage experience is always worth a hearing.

A life-long friend of Cynthia was John Fryatt, who joined the D'Oyly Carte chorus in 1952 and progressed to small parts, then principal roles, which he held until he left to try his hand elsewhere in 1959. Always seemingly behind Neville Griffiths and Leonard Osborn in the principal tenor pecking order, John followed Cynthia to Sadler's Wells, where he quickly established himself in comedy and character parts, particularly in the Offenbach repertoire. Thereafter, John's talents were seen in opera houses all over the world and he was always in demand as a character tenor. At one time, he commuted between the Rome Opera House, where he was appearing in Britten's *The Rake's Progress* and the London Coliseum, to appear as 'Don Basilio' in Mozart's *The Marriage of Figaro* for English National Opera. He was a favourite at Glyndebourne and Cynthia recalls a performance there of Britten's *Peter Grimes*, in which three former D'Oyly Carte principals appeared: Donald Adams, Vivian Tierney and John himself. He also performed at the Royal Opera House, Covent Garden, alongside such stars as Placido Domingo and Kiri Te Kanawa. John was a true singing actor who found his place in the opera world to great effect. He was a charming and delightfully witty man off-stage.

A contemporary of Cynthia and John, Jennifer Toye joined the D'Oyly Carte chorus in 1954 and progressed to become a principal soprano. When she left the company in 1965, she embarked on a varied theatre career, with successful appearances in plays, pantomimes and the famous *Fol de Rols* summer shows. There followed nine months on the high seas as a singer on luxury cruises, which took her from New York to Venezuela, via the Bahamas, Caribbean, Haiti and Puerto Rico. Her final port of call was Sadler's Wells Opera Company, later to become English National Opera, after which she finally settled down and got married. As Jenny points out, like many other performers, she had times when there were gaps between contracts, so she took other jobs including working in wardrobe continuity at Pinewood Studios, which she describes as 'tedious, but handsomely paid'. She also did bar work when necessary and remembers an amusing incident when she and fellow ex-D'Oyly Carter, Eileen Bruckshaw, spotted a familiar face.

'Eileen and I got a job between engagements working at The Comedy Bar pub in London's Haymarket. One evening, Bridget D'Oyly Carte's right-hand man, Albert Truelove, came in and gasped when he saw Eileen. She responded to his surprise with, "You ain't seen nothing yet, Yum-Yum is pulling a pint over there!" Poor Albert was shocked to see us, but why? We had so much fun; it was a great way to meet people and earn a crust before the next gig.'

Such snobbery was typical of the D'Oyly Carte, which obviously expected Miss Carte's young ladies to behave in its prescribed manner even after they had left the company. If working as a barmaid was frowned upon, what the London management would have thought of Maggie Bourgein's next career move can easily be imagined.

Perhaps one of the more unusual appearances by a D'Oyly Carter in a West End musical, Maggie left the company in 1975 to take a part in the erotic show *Oh! Calcutta!*, which called for her to appear nude. During the following D'Oyly Carte London season at Sadler's Wells Theatre, several of her Carte 'friends' (me included) went to see the show. Poor Maggie! In the intervening years, she has recovered from her excruciating embarrassment and forgiven us. She is still working as an actress and writer.

Peggy Ann Jones was one of the most popular soubrettes in the history of the D'Oyly Carte and, on leaving the company in 1973, she embarked on another successful career, appearing in several West End musicals, including *Evita*, *Phantom of the Opera* and the stage adaptation of the cult television comedy, *Dad's Army*. She also appeared in provincial tours of *Fiddler on the Roof* and *Oliver!*. Her film and television credits as an actress are too numerous to list here, but include many well-loved programmes and commercials from the late 1970s through to the 1990s. Despite always seeming to be in work, she assures me that there were times when she was out of a job and in need of something to fill the financial gap. At such times, she called on her skills as a short-hand typist, joining an agency to get temporary work until her next gig. However, it was around the time that this job market was changing towards computerised office systems and Peggy freely admits to being a technophobe.

'Managing new telephones and screens was a nightmare for me and I sometimes walked out of a job rather than be faced with having to type on a computer. But salvation came when I lived in the gorgeous village of Much Hadham in Hertfordshire. My house was right opposite the village pub, The Bull, where I managed to get bar work whenever I needed it. I think they were happy to have me, because I entertained the regulars with my theatre stories. Once a comedienne, always a comedienne! But I never found changing jobs to be a problem. It takes enormous courage and self-belief to walk out of the shadows onto the stage. Being in the spotlight is tough and scary, so finding work outside of the theatre world is easy by comparison with the pressure of being a principal performer. I never minded having to do other jobs, as long as it didn't involve new technology. I'm still as bad today; I'm afraid that computers and I just don't get along, try as I might.'

The number of company members who left to pursue a career in straight theatre was far less than those entering the field of musicals.

Amongst the few was principal comedian, Peter Pratt. On leaving the company in 1959, he embarked on his quest to become an actor in television, theatre and radio with some success. In the 1960s, he was a member of the BBC Drama Repertory Company and also appeared in *A Month in the Country* at London's Cambridge Theatre. In 1976, he took the part of 'The Master' in the iconic television programme, *Doctor Who*, although he would hardly have been recognised, as his character had to wear a thick mask. Between 1969 and 1980, he appeared in the BBC's daily radio soap opera, *Waggoner's Walk*. Peter never lost his love of G&S, appearing in many full productions and concerts, also writing and presenting a play for the BBC called *Jack Point*.

Another D'Oyly Carter to achieve success in the theatre was Dennis Olsen. In 1971, after a year understudying John Reed in the 'patter parts', he returned to his native Australia where, for more than four decades, he has appeared in films, television and drama to great acclaim. Like Peter Pratt, Dennis continued to work in G&S and became hugely popular playing the comedy roles in the Australian Opera's excellent productions of the Savoy Operas.

Probably the most successful D'Oyly Carte singer to turn to straight theatre is Helen Moulder. A New Zealander by birth, she spent a year in the chorus in 1975 before returning home for family reasons. Finding work in her home country proving easier than in Europe, her acting career blossomed over the next forty years and she is still in great demand. Having starred in some fifteen films and numerous theatre and television productions, she is one of New Zealand's best-loved actresses although, of course, she is much too modest to admit it.

'I spent one year with the D'Oyly Carte, as a soprano in the chorus (second fairy from the left). I had come by ship to the UK to do my big Overseas Experience, as we NZers call it, hoping to find work as a singer. Besides travelling in Europe, Scandinavia and Russia, I had done a six-month tour in the chorus of *Rose Marie* and played 'Snow White' in a pantomime in Wales. Then I auditioned for the D'Oyly Carte and when the acceptance letter came, I made a rare and expensive phone call home (at one pound a minute!) to tell my parents, who were over the moon. It was the most exciting thing that had ever happened to me.

'We toured in England and Scotland, played in London and then toured for four months in the USA. I kept my family in touch with all my doings with weekly letters, which I still have. To be part of a famous touring opera company that had existed for so long, with all its traditions, is something I have never forgotten and the experience gave me the confidence to believe I could, perhaps, have a viable career.

'I would have stayed for another year but my mother had been ill, so I decided to go home and see what show business was like in NZ. I had been away for seven years and things had changed, so there were a lot more opportunities for work. My mother had recovered, but I decided to stay and, to my constant surprise, I gradually managed to develop a career in opera, theatre, radio, film and television. In the last twenty years, I have created my own work, writing one and two-person shows, touring them around Australia and New Zealand.

'When I joined the D'Oyly Carte in 1975, the newcomers were rehearsing in London whilst the company was performing at the Royal Festival Hall and we were given tickets to see *The Yeomen of the Guard*, with John Reed as 'Jack Point'. I see, from a letter I sent home, that we all wept buckets at the end. That was the talent of John Reed, from whom I learnt a tremendous amount just being on the stage with him. Given an individual bit of "business" in *Trial by Jury*, I had to stand and wave my hanky at John Reed when he appeared as the judge, before another chorister pulled me back down into my seat. Ridiculous, I know, but it was at that moment, when the audience laughed, that I first experienced the exhilaration of performing comedy, something that has stayed with me all my life.'

Inevitably, there were many D'Oyly Carters who turned their backs on a career in the theatre and found employment in other walks of life. Some combined their careers as performers with other jobs, principal contralto, Patricia Leonard, amongst them. After the closure of the company, Trish was never short of work as a singer. She was a terrific performer and always popular for both concerts and full productions. For nine years, she was a stalwart of the Gawsworth Summer Opera in Cheshire, where open-air G&S played in front of a beautiful Tudor house was great fun. As director of these productions, it was a privilege for me to work with someone so talented. But Trish's husband, Michael Buchan, found work harder to find, so he became a pub landlord in their home town of Stoke-on-Trent. With his wife at his side, they were a formidable partnership for many years. Any D'Oyly Carter who popped in to see them was in for a long session.

The popular 1960s principal tenor, Philip Potter, also went into the pub business, he and his wife running a nine-hundred-year-old ale house in Devon for many years after he retired from the stage. Also taking to the hospitality industry for several years was John Reed, who ran a B&B hotel in Bournemouth with his business partner, Nick Kerry, between his many theatre engagements. I once stayed there and it oozed John's eye for stylish décor, as well as providing an amazing breakfast.

A mezzo-soprano understudy in the 1960s, Abby Hadfield has enjoyed a varied career since leaving the D'Oyly Carte. Between theatre engagements, she worked as a model, was a puppeteer on *The Muppet Show* and ran a boarding kennel in Lincolnshire. Still very much involved as a performer in pantomimes and straight plays, her latest role has been the lead in *Lady in a Van*. Her busy lifestyle and boundless energy notwithstanding, she confesses that, on top of everything else, looking after the cats and dogs in her care is now getting a bit much.

Another choice of work for some of those who had left the company was the retail trade and there are several instances of successful business ventures. To those who knew him, Leonard Osborn, a popular principal tenor in the 1940s and 1950s, with the on-stage charm, elegance and good looks of a true matinee idol, the idea of him running a Post Office for many years seems unlikely to say the least, but so it happened. Always a somewhat aloof man, it is hard to imagine him enjoying banter with regular customers, but it is probable that he was pleasantness personified behind a counter. It is rumoured that, at one time, Leonard ran a laundry, but it has not been possible to verify this.

In 1975, David Porter left the D'Oyly Carte chorus at the same time as his wife, principal soprano, Pamela Field. Living in their native South Wales, whilst Pam continued her theatre career, David set up an electronics firm which he successfully ran for many years. Linda D'Arcy, who spent three years from 1976 as a chorister, went on to open a cafe on the south coast which, I understand, she runs to this day. Following the closure of the D'Oyly Carte, James Conroy-Ward's nigh-impossible task of replacing John Reed as principal comedian left him with little desire to continue in the theatre. Redundancy payment gave him space to consider his future and he eventually took a job with a publishing company in London, remaining with the firm until retirement. However, it is interesting that he has now returned to theatre work, coaching singers at English National Opera and the Royal Opera, Covent Garden, where he started his career. Teaching performers the skills needed for comedy and character acting, in which he excelled, brings him great satisfaction, not to mention free tickets for any operas he fancies seeing.

The caring profession has seen several ex-D'Oyly Carte ladies making a living. When she left the company in 1973, chorister, Kathryn Holding trained to be a nurse, a career she enjoyed for many years. Small-part player and soprano understudy, Marjorie Williams, who spent six years with the D'Oyly Carte from 1969, worked with the elderly in North Lincolnshire until her retirement. Another soprano from the 1970s, Patricia Rea, became interested in the welfare of mentally handicapped children when her own son was born with Downs Syndrome. She has worked tirelessly in this field, running groups in London to support families with disabled young people and, having trained in the Steiner education method, she is as busy as ever.

When Alan Barrett, Mary Sansom and George Cook ended their company careers, they cashed in on their experience working in the Savoy Operas. In 1963, Alan became tired of the Savoy Hill management giving some of his roles to new members, so decided it was time to move on. A year later his wife, Mary, suffered a similar fate when the parts of 'Josephine' in *HMS Pinafore* and 'Elsie Maynard' in *The Yeomen of the Guard* were taken from her and handed over to newcomer, Ann Hood. She, too, decided to leave and together, she and Alan set up a company, Barrett's of Bath, supplying theatrical costumes to amateur companies around the UK. It was a highly successful business, which they ran until they retired.

George Cook was always a dab hand at mending the fans used in *The Mikado* when over-enthusiastic twirling from the men's chorus caused them to break. Everyone with tattered fan vanes handed them over to George for repair. In 1969, he left the company after a successful fifteen-year career playing many of the small bass-baritone roles and understudying Kenneth Sandford. His expertise in making and maintaining fans served him well for over twenty years, seeing him supply not only the D'Oyly Carte with *Mikado* fans, but also amateur groups throughout Great Britain and abroad. When it came to fans, he was the 'Go-To' person in more ways than one.

But it was not just the singers who needed to find work when they left the company. Members of the management, along with music and backstage staff, also needed to look for employment when they left their D'Oyly Carte posts. Peter Riley joined the company as Baggage Master at the tender age of seventeen in 1964 and ended up as Company Manager via all jobs technical. He was devastated when the company closed down. Leaving the D'Oyly Carte was not at all what he wanted, so he came up with ideas to bring back the company he loved so much, as he explains.

'When we closed down the company in 1982, I was asked to assume the role of General Manager to replace Frederic Lloyd, who had retired. As it turned out, I would be General Manager of nothing, as there was nothing left. Between the closure in February and my departure the following September, there wasn't even a meeting of the trustees. I came up with suggestions as to how we could form a new company, writing many notes to Dame Bridget D'Oyly Carte and the trustees, which amounted to nothing. So, in sheer frustration, I resigned my post. So where next?

'Following the company's participation in the Oscar-winning movie, *Chariots of Fire*, David (now Lord) Puttnam told me that if I ever needed a job, he would be more than willing to find something for me, so I got in touch with him and was offered work with the film company, "Goldcrest". However, anxious to hedge my bets, I told David that I had an interview with Louis Benjamin, chairman of Stoll Moss Theatres, and that I would make a decision within twenty-four hours. When I saw Louis, he told me that the Bristol Hippodrome was up for grabs and asked if I was interested – you bet I was! I knew nothing about the film industry, but I knew the Hippodrome, I liked Bristol, so what more could I ask? All went well until Stoll Moss sold the Hippodrome to Apollo Leisure whereupon it became clear that we were not going to get on, so I resigned my position in January of 1985.

'After that, I was lucky to be head-hunted for the position of Managing Director of the Gaiety Theatre in Dublin, a position I accepted on a six-month trial basis but, for various reasons, it didn't work out, so I returned home and teamed up with an old friend who ran a pub in Oldbury-on-Severn, near Bristol. After a period of training, I became a partner/manager and this lasted for six years, after which I took a pub of my own for two years and then a hotel in Clifton for six years. Thereafter, I returned to "normal" life, something new for me, and took a job with a health care logistics company until my retirement in 2012. Bored with nothing to do after I had completed all the jobs that needed doing around the house, I took a part-time job with the car rental firm, Avis, which I am still doing.'

Despite his eventual departure from the theatre world, Peter remains a theatrical at heart and, like many ex-D'Oyly Carters, still has a passion for his life with the company which meant so much to him. One of Peter's colleagues on the Stage Management team in the 1970s, Ken Robertson-Scott, has remained in the world of entertainment and enjoyed a spell as a BBC television director. One of his credits was the long-running children's programme, *Chucklevision*, for which Ken brought in several of his Carte colleagues to play roles in the comedy show. One episode featured principal soprano, Julia Goss, as an opera diva and myself as a theatre cleaner in a story of mistaken identity. Called *Gala Performance*, it can still be found on YouTube and is not to be missed!

After leaving the BBC, Ken developed a career as a freelance lighting designer and is still in demand today. He also went into stage direction, with many credits for amateur productions of G&S and musicals. However, like Peter Riley, he retained his love for the D'Oyly Carte. He became the Technical Director of *The Magic of Gilbert and Sullivan*, the successful concert group formed by company performers on the closure of the ill-fated company. He was vital to the running and organisation of this group as a member of its board of trustees. Happily, there have not been too many dark spots in his career.

It is probably true to say that, over the years, most members of the D'Oyly Carte's music staff remained involved in the industry in some way after leaving the company. A notable exception was Isidore Godfrey OBE, who left the company in 1968 after thirty-nine years as Music Director. After such a lengthy tenure, it is hardly surprising that he chose to retire and live a quiet life. His successor, James Walker, left after three years and returned to his previous job, producing classical music records for Decca. Following him was Royston Nash. On leaving the D'Oyly Carte in 1979, he crossed the pond to become the conductor of the Cape Cod Symphony Orchestra in Massachusetts, a post he held until 2007. Fraser Goulding, who succeeded Royston, has conducted orchestras throughout the UK since the company's closure. Others of the music staff who are still active include repetiteur, Paul Seeley, now a respected musicologist and author.

We have seen that the careers of some D'Oyly Carters took unexpected turns when they left the company but, perhaps, Clive Harre's story is one of the most unusual. Clive, the last baritone to captain *HMS Pinafore*, was devastated to find himself made redundant when the company folded. For the next few years, he managed to eke out a living as a performer but, eventually, he found himself without a gig.

'There I was in 1990, out of work. Most of the preceding years had been spent on the road, so I did not relish the idea of working in an office. One day, as I was walking into town, a bus passed me and I saw an advert on the back of it. This said, "Drivers required". I took down the telephone number and made a call when I got home. I was invited to the garage and told I would be given an assessment. On the day arranged, I parked my car and went inside, where the instructor told me we were to go on a test drive. As I started to walk back to my car, he said, "Oy! Where do you think you're going?" In all innocence I replied, "To my car. You wanted to see how I drive." He pointed and said, "Don't be daft, you're going to drive one of these." It was a double decker omnibus!

'Into the cab I climbed and, by this time, my legs were like jelly. I started the engine and off we went around Purfleet, in what I can only describe as country lanes. For about fifty minutes, I drove the damn thing, praying to Our Lord that nothing would come the other way! Eventually, we returned to the garage, with me dripping with perspiration, to be told, "You'll do. Report on Monday at 8.30am to start your training." I passed my test first time and was soon out ferrying passengers on the roads of Romford and Ilford. I didn't think I would last a week, but I did, right up until October of 2010, when I was forced to take early retirement due to the onset of Parkinson's Disease. I must say that, once I had gained my confidence, I enjoyed the job very much indeed.'

Another baritone to happen upon a career change by accident was Paul Waite. Having joined the D'Oyly Carte in 1973 as a chorister, small-part player and understudy to Kenneth Sandford, Paul happily embraced company life and thoroughly enjoyed his work, particularly any opportunities to deputise for Ken. But, after a few years, his enthusiasm waned and he began to get itchy feet.

'I felt I was nearing the end of my time with the company and, after four and a half years of G&S, I was beginning to feel restless; a change of direction in life was calling. At the time, I had no idea what that change would be, but I knew it would not be with the D'Oyly Carte Opera Company. Word must have got out that my understudy performances had been well-received, because I found out that the General Manager, Frederic Lloyd, and Bridget D'Oyly Carte wanted to see me in action, so they came to see one of my appearances as 'Wilfred Shadbolt' in *Yeomen*. One day soon after, I was summoned to an interview with Freddie Lloyd at the Savoy Hotel. I couldn't think why on earth he would want to see me but, apparently, he had heard that I was intending to move on and was hoping to persuade me otherwise.

'During the interview, Freddie was very keen to let me know how well he thought I had done covering four of Ken Sandford's roles at Sadler's Wells Theatre and elsewhere. He talked about the imminent tour of America as a good reason for staying on. It was a very difficult interview for me, because the General Manager was trying to persuade me to remain with the company, whilst I was increasingly feeling like a tightly-coiled spring about to snap if I didn't leave soon. I couldn't bring myself to say that to his face and tell him that the real reason I wanted to leave was because I'd had enough so, instead, I pointed out that it didn't look like Ken was going anywhere soon, to which Freddie replied, "Well, Mr Waite, I'm afraid we can't push Mr Sandford under a bus."

'I left the company soon after that interview, but I hadn't a clue what I was going to do. As it turned out, a series of dead-end jobs until, one day, I discovered carpentry and joinery whilst delivering parcels to a huge joinery firm in Feltham, West London. That was the beginning of my immersion into a whole new realm of working with wood as a professional carpenter and joiner, which put bread on the table and kept a roof over my head for the next thirty-five years. My life has

116

always been driven by passion and when the passion stops, it's time for a change.'

As for me, I am lucky enough to still be working in the theatre world. When the D'Oyly Carte closed down, I had no clue as to what to do next and having to sign on for unemployment benefit seemed like the end of my world after ten years of regular work. It took time to find my feet, but working as a walk-on and small-part artist in television, along with selling lottery tickets for West Bromwich Albion football club kept the wolf from the door until I gradually began to pick up work as a director for amateur operatic societies all over the country. Thereafter, performing took a back seat as my career as a stage director, on both sides of the Atlantic, kept me busy and I felt I had found my niche.

Amateur shows may have been my staple fare, but directing shows for the Gawsworth Summer Opera and at the International Gilbert and Sullivan Festival brought the opportunity of working with D'Oyly Carte principals including Valerie Masterson, Gillian Knight, Peggy Ann Jones, Julia Goss, Patricia Leonard, Lorraine Daniels, Kenneth Sandford, John Ayldon, Michael Rayner and Geoffrey Shovelton. What a privilege and joy it was. Imagine my first principal rehearsal for *HMS Pinafore* in Berkeley, California, for the American leg of the G&S Festival in 1997. In front of me sat Valerie, Gillian and Kenneth, which was a little bit intimidating to say the least. All I could do was take a deep breath, try to look as if I knew what I was doing and pray that my work would pass muster with such legendary Savoyards. Happily, I survived to tell the tale. Also, my involvement, both on and off the stage, with *The Magic of Gilbert and Sullivan* group brought me many years of happiness. To be singing again with D'Oyly Carte colleagues was such a pleasure. I still miss the wonderful concerts we staged around the UK and, in particular, the annual Festive Season concerts in London, Birmingham and Manchester, when company fans flocked to see their favourite G&S performers once more.

Like most theatrical folk, I have had some blips along the way when work was intermittent and it was during one quiet spell, some fifteen years ago, that a chance conversation led to me taking part-time work, the first 'proper job' I had ever done. It was summertime, often a barren period for directing shows, when a friend mentioned

117

that she was working in a popular cafe in Pwllheli, just a few miles from where I live. Talked into joining her for the busy summer season, I thoroughly enjoyed the new experience and stayed on – and on. The cafe is now a smart bistro-style eatery and I can still be found there on most Monday evenings, when live jazz packs in the locals. When away from my Welsh home, perhaps directing a show, or on a regular trip to America to give performance Master Classes, my colleagues in the cafe always welcome me back, quite literally, with open arms. I wouldn't change it for anything.

Whether they continued working in the theatre, or made a very different career choice, most ex-D'Oyly Carters have happy memories of their time with the company. Indeed, many of those who remained in the business acknowledge the positive influence of the Gilbert and Sullivan repertoire on their development as performers. Anyone who thinks G&S is lightweight and easy should think again. We who have benefited from D'Oyly Carte careers know the truth.

CHAPTER SEVEN

FAQ

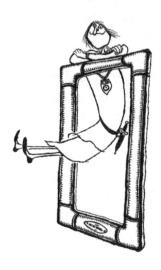

The fascination of the D'Oyly Carte Opera Company for its many fans around the world lay not only in the appeal of its famous performers and the wonderful works of Gilbert and Sullivan, but also in the detail of how such a unique theatrical organisation operated. Being asked about the minutiae of company life was something that every D'Oyly Carter experienced. Sometimes, questions could be intrusive and too personal for comfort, so diplomacy was the order of the day when confronted by an enthusiastic fan but, generally, the thirst for information was, and still is, a genuine desire to learn about what went on behind the scenes of such a large touring repertory company. For those D'Oyly Carte aficionados too young to have seen the company before its demise in 1982 and for others who are still curious, some of the most frequently asked questions are now answered.

How did the D'Oyly Carte transport its effects and personnel?

Before the 1960s, the company relied on rail transport to carry its performers, scenery, costumes and props around the United Kingdom. From the earliest days of the D'Oyly Carte in the late 1870s, several of the Savoy Operas could be in the touring repertoire, so a complete train was hired to take everything and everyone from one date to another. A local haulage firm would be engaged to collect sets, boxes and crates from the theatre and get them to the railway station, with another firm awaiting the train's arrival to reverse this procedure. Arrangements having to be made in advance by the management, it was a massive year-round job to get the company around the country.

By the 1960s, the development of road transport links saw the gradual phasing out of the Sunday train call ritual, as the D'Oyly Carte turned to large lorries to take everything from town-to-town. Increasing numbers of the company's performers and staff owning cars meant that there was no longer any need to dress formally, as required by the management, for the train journey, which was seen as a major departure for the better. Somewhat sadly, the traditions associated with train calls, such as chorus, principals and staff travelling in separate carriages, card schools, picnics, alcoholic conviviality and companionship passed into memory.

If the logistics of moving a touring opera company within the UK were difficult enough, how much more so for overseas tours? Before the age of air travel, the D'Oyly Carte's regular North American tours meant having to convey the company across the Atlantic by ship. With everything required for the operas to be played in the States and Canada safely stored in the hold, company members could look forward to a welcome few days off, although it can be imagined that those who suffered from sea-sickness did not enjoy the experience in the event of a rough crossing.

By the mid-1950s, the London management was quick to see the advantage of using readily available commercial flights to America to get the company across the Atlantic in a fraction of the time of going by sea. Although taking much longer than modern jet aircraft, the journey was usually managed within a day or two, depending on destination, meaning a considerable saving in transport costs and travel time. It can be supposed that arranging with airlines the storage of sets, costumes and props in the hold of the plane was no mean feat in the early days of D'Oyly Carte air travel. In fact, Peter Riley can attest to the challenges he sometimes faced getting everything for the operas to and from America.

'At the end of the 1968 Central City season, the operas we did there were being sent by road to Baltimore for shipping by sea back to England, but the three weeks it was going to take meant that everything would not arrive back in our London stores in time for any remedial work on costumes, scenery and props to be done during the upcoming four-week vacation period. So, I had to separate all the items in need of attention and the only way to get them back was to fly them. We had chartered a Canadair CL44 to get the company home and I figured out that there would be sufficient room on the aircraft to accommodate everything needing repair. So, everything was loaded into the hold, where possible, but some items wouldn't fit, so they were carried in the passenger compartment, including my office skip, which contained the necessary customs manifests for absolutely everything.

'The aircraft had so much weight on it that, when it came to take off from Denver, it didn't seem as if we were going to make it! What didn't help was that company members had bought so many souvenirs from Central City that the weight of personal baggage was astronomical. As a result, we had to make a refuelling stop in Gander to get us across the Atlantic, so the flight lasted seventeen hours. That was bad enough, but there was only one stewardess on board and very little food. Needless to say, we ran out of alcohol as well!

'Prior to our departure, the company was enjoying a farewell celebration at the Teller House Hotel in Central City, when I received news that the plane was delayed and would not arrive until the following morning. As everyone had packed up and checked out of their accommodation in the town, we had to make arrangements for them to stay over another night. And quite a night it turned out to be, with many sore heads on the flight the following morning! However, because family and friends had made arrangements to meet company members on our arrival back at Gatwick, I had to obtain their contact details to let them know of the delay. Albert Truelove and I spent most of the night at the telephone switchboard of the Chain of Mines Hotel getting in touch about the delayed flight with those expecting to meet their nearest and dearest. It was an incident I shall never forget!'

This may seem hard to believe, but I can remember being told by long-time chorister Beti Lloyd-Jones about people with hangovers stumbling over pieces of scenery stacked along the aisle as they tried to stretch their legs during that long flight. Only the D'Oyly Carte! Despite such perils, there was no going back to travelling across the Atlantic by ship.

The final overseas tour undertaken by the company in 1979 was its only one to Australia and New Zealand. The three-month sea trip it took to get sets, costumes, wigs and props Down Under meant that *HMS Pinafore* and *Iolanthe* had to be taken out of the UK tour dates. Fortunately, the D'Oyly Carte had two *Mikado* sets, so one was used at home whilst the other was in transit and costumes were able to be taken on the company flight to Oz. Once there, Company Manager, Peter Riley, had the added nightmare of trying to get the scenery to New Zealand and back to Australia again, because planes flying the necessary routes were not big enough to take all the sets. All through the D'Oyly Carte's long history of touring so many shows, audiences who flocked to see their favourite Gilbert and Sullivan operettas would have had little idea of the marathon task of transporting everything needed to present them with a performance in their local theatre. But why should they? It was not part of the magic.

What happened to the sets and costumes when the company closed?

The simple answer is that some of the sets were destroyed, some were sold and most of the costumes were sent to auction. Peter Riley recalls that the impresario, Richard Condon, who was put in charge of the revival of the D'Oyly Carte in 1987, had some of the scenery repainted for use in the professional pantomimes he produced, but everything that was not sold on was broken up and dumped. When one thinks of the simple, but functional scenery that was, over so many years, the setting for thousands of eagerly-anticipated performances, it seems a pity that all of the sets could not have been saved, but there was no room for sentimentality in the new company.

Former Carte Stage Manager, Ken Robertson-Scott, was party to the sale of some of the sets by the New D'Oyly Carte and relates that the scenery for *HMS Pinafore* was sold to Martin McEvoy Productions for a tour. Ken was responsible for erecting the scenery, but after a performance in Leicester, the lorry carrying the set was involved in a serious accident and most of it was destroyed. However, that was not the only sale in which he played a part, as he explains.

'The Disley Jones *Mikado* set was sold to the Penzance Gilbert and Sullivan Society and then to the Plymouth Gilbert and Sullivan Society. I fitted it up in both towns, before it was sold to a set rental company because it was too big for most amateur societies to use. It was later destroyed in a fire. The sets for *Iolanthe* and *Princess Ida* were sold to the Plymouth group before being bought by the Houston Gilbert and Sullivan Society in Texas, where they remain to this day. Both have been used on two or three occasions. I think the *Ida* set is, probably, the oldest in the world, as it is now sixty-five years old.'

According to Peter Riley, the company's Camberwell stores, in South London, were sold off after the death of Dame Bridget D'Oyly Carte in 1985, as part of her estate. The building was bought by a firm making theatrical drapes and stage cloths in the upstairs areas, formerly the Carte's wardrobe department. Another firm, which dealt in theatre hardware, bought the lower floor, which had housed the company's scenery. For anyone new to the D'Oyly Carte in the 1960s and 1970s, the visits to the wardrobe department to be fitted for their costumes by Ruby Buckingham will be clearly remembered. It was an Aladdin's cave of fabrics, cutting tables and busy sewing stations, which induced a sense of excitement for the new job ahead. It was the place where costumes for all of the operas were cleaned and refurbished at the end of every tour. Sometimes, new costumes were made for those joining but, mostly, they were given a costume that had been used by several previous performers. My own costume for *The Yeomen of the Guard* was somewhat threadbare when I inherited it in 1972 and the name tag of its previous occupant could be traced back to the 1940s. For a company operating on a tight budget, nothing was wasted and many the principal who wore with pride the costume bearing the name of an illustrious predecessor.

In the late summer of 1988, the sale of the company's costumes and props was arranged by Albert Truelove, who had been the Personal Secretary to Dame Bridget D'Oyly Carte. The idea of raising money towards a re-launch for the defunct company by selling its wardrobe and effects had been discussed for some time before the Dame's death in 1985, but Peter Riley says that she was very unhappy at the prospect at selling off everything, but was probably too ill by then to do much about it. A decision was made to keep some individual military uniforms, the beautiful set of *Iolanthe* peers' robes and *Yeomen* warders' uniforms, later used for the New D'Oyly Carte productions, but everything else was to go. The sale was handled by the prestigious London auctioneers, Christies, but the large influx of money anticipated by the company's trustees did not materialise. As it turned out, the big sell-off was mainly attended by fans seeking souvenirs of their favourite performers, which they got at knock-down prices, with costumiers buying various garments to add to their stock and collectors of G&S memorabilia picking up bargains. The sale of props was no more successful as Peter explains.

'I know that the camel we used in the 1975 production of *Utopia Limited* was sold for a measly five pounds and when it was made it cost us about five hundred.' That prop camel was, by the by, nicknamed 'Arfa' by company members, because it had only one side, the side that faced the audience! Said camel can be seen on the cover of the D'Oyly Carte's 1976 recording of *Utopia Limited* bearing Kenneth Sandford as 'King Paramount'.

It is worth noting that some thirty D'Oyly Carte costumes are part of Melvin Tarran's personal collection of G&S memorabilia. For many years, his extensive collection, the world's largest permanent display, was housed at Oak Hall in Sussex, but since Melvin sold the house to the National Trust, it is awaiting a new home. An interesting story of a D'Oyly Carte costume making an unexpected appearance, fifteen years after the closure of the company, came about on the American leg of the International Gilbert and Sullivan Festival in 1997. A long-time fan of Kenneth Sandford, who lived in the States, had bought Ken's 'Sir Despard Murgatroyd' first act costume and offered it to him for the performances of *Ruddigore* at the festival. Ken, who was surprised and delighted to find that it still fitted him, was once again able to strut his melodramatic stuff in familiar garb. Whilst Ken and I were directing the Gawsworth Summer Opera in Cheshire, we made a visit to a costumier in Manchester and I remember us feeling very sad to see some immediately identifiable D'Oyly Carte costumes squashed unceremoniously on rails amongst cheap, nondescript outfits. It was a poignant moment indeed.

Why did the Arts Council withdraw its funding to the D'Oyly Carte?

This question has probably been asked more than any other and it continues to be asked to this day. Former D'Oyly Carters have regularly been faced with this query and the answer still surprises those who ask. Public outrage that such a famous opera company was forced to close down, after more than a century of success, was rife after the closure. Righteous indignation led to scathing attacks on the Arts Council for allowing it to happen, but this criticism was entirely without foundation. The D'Oyly Carte never received funding from the Arts Council, nor any other public body. It was a business which survived entirely on its Box Office receipts until the cost of touring so many shows became too great for it to continue.

When the company's perilous financial position became apparent to the management, the D'Oyly Carte Opera Trust made an application to the Arts Council for funding to allow its operation to continue. An offer was made, but the attached conditions were deemed unacceptable to the die-hard traditionalists amongst the trustees, who would only accept the money if it allowed the company to carry on operating as it had always done. The Arts Council's offer was conditional on, amongst other things, reducing the number of shows in the repertoire and the inclusion of operettas other than Gilbert and Sullivan. With enough of the trustees against such a departure, the offer was refused and so, despite fund-raising measures which amounted to very little, the end was inevitable. This explanation of the true facts has always been greeted with amazement: the finger of blame has always been pointed in the wrong direction.

How did performers on tour cope in the event of illness?

With eight performances every week, keeping well was always a worry for D'Oyly Carte performers, particularly for principals who carried the responsibility of not letting down audiences. For them, a heavy cold and cough could make singing at their usual high level almost impossible. Although reluctant to miss a performance, it sometimes could not be avoided and their understudies had to go on. For choristers, it was much easier to perform when feeling under the weather. Singing with a head cold was manageable, but a bad sore throat and chest was another matter. Most people usually recovered within a few days and normal service was resumed but, occasionally, medical attention was necessary. If any company member needed the services of a doctor when away from home, the first port of call was the theatre notice board, where the contact numbers of medical professionals willing to treat travelling theatricals were available. In the event of being off work for more than a few days, performers could get from them the sick notes required by the company management as proof of illness.

In the event of long-term illness, as occasionally happened, the company had either to manage without a sick performer, or find a temporary replacement. The management was, generally, very supportive of those who were ill and there are many instances of Bridget D'Oyly Carte taking a personal interest in her performers who were seriously ill. It was not unknown for her to pay for private medical consultations to help them towards a speedy recovery, go to visit them, or send them on recuperative holidays.

Performers with chronic medical conditions which needed them to make regular hospital visits had to make their own arrangements for the treatment they required. Knowing in advance the towns and cities where the company would be appearing was essential to enable them to contact hospitals and book appointments. Meston Reid, who was a principal tenor in the final years of the company, suffered from a blood condition which needed regular monitoring, so it was part of his touring routine to make sure he got in touch with local hospitals well-ahead of time to make sure he got his necessary treatment. If this was complicated for him in the UK, how much more so when touring abroad? In the present day of instant communications and the internet, researching hospitals in such far-flung places as New Zealand is easy enough, but not so in 1979. Being ill happened to every D'Oyly Carter from time-to-time, but the shows always went on one way or another.

What happened at times of family bereavement?

The D'Oyly Carte management was clear in its policy of allowing time off for performers affected by bereavement. Only in cases of a close family member dying were they allowed time to make arrangements, or attend funerals. Even then, unless there were unusual circumstances, they were only allowed a short period away from work. Anyone other than a spouse, parent or child was not considered close enough, so many company members experienced the sadness of missing the funeral of a grandparent, aunt, uncle, cousin or friend. Sometimes, those who had lost someone close could be hundreds, or even thousands, of miles away when a death occurred, meaning a long journey to attend the funeral. The shock of a phone call to the theatre conveying the news of the death of a family member was always horrible for anyone who had to go on for a performance but, somehow, go on they did. It was at such times that the D'Oyly Carte family pulled together to help and console those suffering the grief of being bereaved. When far away from home and family, the care and support of their colleagues helped them get through the worst moments.

How did the D'Oyly Carte pay its performers?

Speaking to company members who were with the D'Oyly Carte in the 1950s, it has been possible to establish that they were paid weekly, in cash, both at home and abroad. This method of paying salaries continued until the mid-1970s, when the change to payment into individual bank accounts every week was made. This may have suited the management but, for performers used to the welcome knock on the dressing room door from the Business Manager handing out wage packets, having to go to a bank to get cash was not so convenient.

Arrangements to pay the cast and staff during overseas tours were somewhat different. In the days prior to monies being paid into bank accounts, wages were paid every week in the local currency. Thereafter, everyone was allowed to decide how much of their weekly pay they wanted to be paid into their bank accounts at home to cover bills and expenses, with the remainder paid in cash once a week. At the beginning of an overseas tour, a cash advance was paid prior to departure to tide everyone over until their first wage packet was due. Payment for hotel accommodation needed to be considered when deciding how much money to have in hand and what to keep back. Sometimes, there would be a choice of hotels with varying room rates, so company members could judge beforehand the amount of money they would need.

It was certainly a test of money management to be able to survive from week-to-week without ending up strapped for cash. The temptation to buy souvenirs was always there, so it was easy to overspend. For those on their first tour abroad, the cost of eating out every day also had to be taken into consideration and it was not unknown for small loans to be sought from more careful colleagues until pay day. In my experience, touring in North America, Australia and New Zealand was no time for frugality for those of us who were single; we were handed the opportunity to see the world and most of us seized it, hoping we had correctly judged how much we could spend without getting into financial difficulty. However, it was different for performers with families, who needed to make sure those at home received sufficient money to keep them going for the duration of an overseas tour.

Did the D'Oyly Carte have company warm-ups?

Unlike some professional companies, the D'Oyly Carte left warming up for shows to the performers. The practice of getting singers together for a joint warm-up has always been common in professional music theatre and many amateur groups do the same, but the Carte, certainly in its latter years, did not consider this necessary. Principals were well-aware that warming up the voice with a series of vocal exercises was essential to a good performance, so they got on with it in the privacy of their dressing rooms, or in the toilet if they were sharing a room. The idiosyncrasies of individual preparation were instantly recognisable to anyone passing dressing room doors, but the many strange sounds emanating from behind them, fortunately, belied the final product. Principal sopranos and tenors were, generally, the noisiest, but everyone had their own method. Patter man, James Conroy-Ward, a fine bass singer, made the most ghastly sounds when getting ready to go on. Of course, there were exceptions and John Reed was notorious for not bothering to warm up, his familiar cry of 'Hip bath, hip bath! Yes, it's there,' being well-known to everyone. For choristers playing small roles, the opportunity to warm up was limited to the toilet, because vocalising in the dressing room was not the done thing. In a show such as *The Gondoliers*, with so many small roles played by choristers, the idea of them all doing scales and arpeggios at the same time was unthinkable.

A communal warm-up, apart from bringing a sense of readiness before a performance, gives the Music Director the chance to put right any slipshod musical details, but the D'Oyly Carte always did things its own way. If something in the music needed to be addressed, the conductor went to dressing rooms to give his notes. There may well have been a practical reason why the performers did not warm up together. The Carte was, predominantly, a touring company and warm-ups would have needed a piano to be readily available in every theatre. This was not as straightforward as it sounds, because many provincial theatres did not have rehearsal room facilities with ready access to a piano. Despite such disadvantages, principals armed with tuning forks and pitch pipes managed to get their vocal cords ready for work, but it has to be admitted that most of the choristers used the opening chorus to get their voices going.

How did the principals keep their work fresh?

Having to perform the same operas scores of times every year was a challenge for all D'Oyly Carte principals, the problem of avoiding becoming stale a constant factor. Most of them saw this repetition as an opportunity to improve their interpretations of Gilbert's words and Sullivan's music. For senior principals who spent over a quarter of a century with the company, it is hard to imagine that they could find previously unexplored nuances in their characterisations, but they did, taking pleasure in finding something new to add to their work. Kenneth Sandford was well-known for grumbling that he never really got 'Pooh-Bah', in *The Mikado*, as he would have liked. Always looking for something extra to add to his performance, such humility and dedication to his work would have astounded audiences, most of whom saw his interpretation of the 'Lord High Everything Else' as definitive.

For dialogue scenes, performers often got their heads together to explore possibilities, something that, usually, went unnoticed by the company's artistic directors. That they cared about their work to such an extent is a tribute to their artistry and professionalism. They, more than anyone, understood that W.S. Gilbert offered far more to an actor than is generally perceived. Dig beneath the surface of, seemingly, superficial characters and it is possible to find real people with complex human traits: that was Gilbert's genius. Searching out detail was what kept performances fresh.

Understandably, principals and choristers alike sometimes got fed up with doing the same shows over and over again, so in-jokes and pranks that bypassed the audience were common; it was a survival mechanism that made the repetitive nature of their work more fun. Never will those of us on the stage during a performance of *Mikado*, when John Ayldon, playing the title role, found himself in possession of a pair of bicycle clips around the bottom of his trousers, forget the stifled hilarity, or the look on John's face when he saw the addition to his costume. The work of two wicked chorus ladies kneeling in front of him, with their backs to the audience, who were able to place the clips around his ankles as he passed by them during his second act song, it was a prime example of having some fun without compromising the show. Blacked-out teeth were always good for a laugh, particularly in the Act Two finale of *Patience*, when the 'Duke of Dunstable' once invited the ladies to "Approach such of you who are truly lovely". The girls, unnoticed by the audience, gave him a gummy grin that corpsed the poor Duke! Juvenile behaviour, yes, but it must be understood that such practical jokes were never seen by the audience. Every workplace needs some levity and the D'Oyly Carte was no exception.

What was it like to forget the words?

Given that the D'Oyly Carte Opera Company gave not far short of four hundred performances every year, occurrences of performers forgetting their lines, or 'drying' as it is known in the business, were mercifully few. However conscientious they were in going through their lines prior to a performance, most principals occasionally experienced the distress of losing the words. Anyone who has been through that moment when the mind goes blank will say that it is horrible. The time it takes for a prompt to come may only be a matter of seconds, but the disconcerting silence seems to go on forever. As the D'Oyly Carte never employed a 'prompt', it was down to colleagues to feed the missing lines, or ad-lib until the panicky performer opposite them picked up the thread again. This worked well when there was more than one person on the stage, but what happened when a performer working alone on the stage dried up? Losing the words to an aria was usually put right by a prompt from the conductor with the music in front of him, but he could not necessarily be relied on to supply a chunk of missing dialogue. In this case, it was down to the lonely soloist to find a way out of their self-inflicted dilemma. When all else failed, going to the prompt corner to take a look at the Stage Manager's libretto was the only solution, not something that happened very often.

The embarrassment felt on forgetting lines was sometimes compounded by audience members helpfully offering the missing words. Most D'Oyly Carte front-row fans knew the dialogue and music as well as those on the stage above them, instantly noticing a missing dotted crotchet, note held too long or paraphrased line. Irritating maybe, but it was an occupational hazard. Doing so many performances of the same operas at least meant that principals became familiar with the lines of all the characters in the scenes they played, so it was usually possible for them to feed a line to a colleague who had gone blank, or improvise something to jog their memory. It was said that performers who knew each other's work very well could recognise a certain look in the eyes of those struggling for their next line before it happened. Once in the wings, grateful thanks were waved away by those who never knew when they might need the favour returned. It happened to the best.

Sometimes, an unfortunate slip of the tongue could bring hilarity for performers and audience alike, but it was more usual for those watching to feel uncomfortable when a lengthy silence occurred on the stage. There are far too many tales of D'Oyly Carte principals drying up to relate here; suffice it to say that they would not, very likely, be happy to be reminded. I can, however, share an experience of me wondering what the hell came next.

Whenever contralto understudy Beti Lloyd-Jones went on as the 'Duchess of Plaza Toro', in *The Gondoliers*, I deputised for her as 'Inez'. It is often said that playing small roles is not an easy option and 'Inez' is a prime example of a 'banana skin part'. While all the other principals have done their work for the evening, poor old 'Inez' has to make her entrance at the very end of the opera to deliver the denouement tidying up the complications of who is the real King of Barataria. It was a nerve-racking moment waiting to come on to find every eye on both sides of the footlights firmly fixed on you but, usually, I was fine once on the stage. Ken Sandford, as 'Don Alhambra del Bolero' came to meet me and always whispered the same nonsense about being sure to tell everyone what he had told me in the torture chamber and off I would go. However, on one occasion, everything went as normal, with Ken leading me to a seat and encouraging me to get on with it, until I opened my mouth to sing. My opening line was nowhere. I can remember the veil of panic descending as I tried to think but, while I racked my brains, I was aware of my voice delivering the lines as normal. It was the strangest thing. That my brain was doing two things in a split second was quite unnerving and I have never forgotten the feeling of relief when I pronounced 'Luiz' to be the rightful king.

Did the performers get lots of free tickets?

The answer to this question is no. The D'Oyly Carte had a strict policy of only occasionally allowing its staff to have complimentary seats, or 'comps' as they are known in the theatre world. For prestigious performances, such as the Last Night of a London season, everyone was, usually, allowed two free tickets. If anyone wanted comps for other performances, for example, if they were appearing in their home town and wanted family members to come to a show, it was a case of making a request to the touring manager and hoping for the best. Providing this did not happen too often, a couple of tickets would be forthcoming. Company members respected this and were always grateful to be given free seats. Of course, this was during my time in the D'Oyly Carte, but Cynthia Morey, who was in the company in the 1950s, tells me that, in those days, she cannot remember anyone getting comps; they had to pay for any tickets they wanted.

It was not that the management was mean, more that, as a repertory company touring without public funding, tickets needed to be sold rather than given away. Apart from small amounts from corporate sponsors, Box Office revenue was the company's sole means of income, so it was vital to sell as many seats as possible. In most towns and cities, audience attendance was very good and tickets were

132

in great demand, so giving them away was not an option. Having said that, it is worth mentioning that on the rare occasions that the opening performance of a run was not well-sold, it was common to give away seats, particularly to the press, in order to provide an audience and encourage attendance on other nights, a practice known as 'papering' and backstage word went round that it was a 'paper audience'.

Do ex-D'Oyly Carte performers still get royalties?

Yes, but not very often and only in small amounts. Since the company closed down nearly forty years ago, public interest in its recordings has gradually diminished to the point where money accruing to extant performers has dwindled to next-to-nothing. Within twenty years of its beginning in 1875, the D'Oyly Carte Opera Company was issuing recordings of the Savoy Operas using the new acoustical technology and it continued to release records on a regular basis until the late 1970s. Whenever new recording techniques were developed, the company took advantage of improved sound quality to release records showcasing their current stars. Even after closure, old company recordings have been re-mastered and digitalised for present-day listeners, but the small number of Carte performers still entitled to payment for their work now see very little money.

Although much is known about the very earliest recordings, little is known about how company artistes were paid for making them. By the 1960s, the system for distributing royalties was well-established. The trade union representing the acting profession, Equity, collected the money from record sales and sent cheques to its members. But how was the amount due to each performer calculated? When the management announced that a new recording was to be made, principals met to decide, on a points system, how many points each of them should get. The amount varied according to the responsibility of the roles and their seniority within the company. For example, a new principal would not get as many points as their senior colleagues such as John Reed, Kenneth Sandford, Donald Adams, Valerie Masterson and Gillian Knight. It was not unknown for such meetings to become fractious as everyone tried to get the best deal for themselves. A points allowance also had to be made for small roles, usually played by choristers. With a specified percentage of the overall royalties set for equal division amongst the chorus members, the rest was up for grabs and many the peeved principal who felt they should have got more.

When it came to making a recording, everyone was paid a set fee for each session in the studio, so this was always a welcome addition to wages. Thereafter, Equity, having been advised of the points allocation, periodically issued cheques for sales of all recordings in which D'Oyly Carte performers were involved. This is still the case today, although the collection system is slightly different, but those of us now entitled to royalties get quite a shock when a few pennies show up once in a blue moon.

Have company members kept in touch over the years?

Given the close working relationships that were such an important part of touring life, it is no surprise that the friendships which developed between performers have stood the test of time. Even when going their different ways after leaving the D'Oyly Carte, good friends have stayed in touch to this day. There may be times when busy lives lead to gaps in communication, but the thread is never broken. It may be a cliché to talk about the D'Oyly Carte 'family', but it was, and still is, an exclusive club, membership of which is highly prized. Of course, friendships between contemporaries could be expected, but it is not uncommon for company members from different eras to have become friends via the D'Oyly Carte link.

A chance encounter in West Chester, Pennsylvania, when I was on a teaching trip to the States, led to a lasting friendship with chorister, John Dennison. John introduced himself to me after a class, and told me he was living in the university city and had heard that I was going to be in town. He was with the company for just a year after he joined in 1957, but his enthusiasm for his short time with the D'Oyly Carte is astonishing some six decades after he left it to return to America. We see each other every second year, but keep in touch between times and he loves hearing all the news of Carte folk. His close friends in the company were Alan Barrett, Mary Sansom and Anne Sessions, all of whom are now gone, but he will always be a proud D'Oyly Carter. A contemporary of John Dennison from the 1950s is Cynthia Morey, whom I first got to know through her great pal, John Reed. I am lucky to have such friends. During research for my books about the D'Oyly Carte, it has been my pleasure to get to know many people who were with the company before my time and learn about their lasting friendships with colleagues. What is clear is that they remain as important today as they were some sixty years ago and we very much miss those no longer with us.

What was John Reed really like?

For those who were in the company with John, this question was asked of them time and again by fans who knew his stage characters, but wanted to know about the real man. Indisputably, one of the most famous Savoyards of all time, whilst John enjoyed the adulation of his many D'Oyly Carte fans, he valued his privacy. Like any other star performer, John had to put up with more than his fair share of attention at the Stage Door, when it was easy to feel like public property. Whether aimed directly at him, or via his colleagues, interest in every aspect of John's private life often brought impertinent questioning which had to be parried. Adoring women in love with him wanted to know if he was married, ever-hopeful of securing his affections. How old was he? Another frequently asked question. Where did he live? Before the days of the internet, finding out such personal information was not easy, so extreme measures were sometimes taken and, as earlier mentioned, John was deeply hurt when he discovered that a copy of his birth certificate had been circulated at the Stage Door. For all the great D'Oyly Carte principals, being so popular with audiences had its downside. Constant, prying attention went with the territory: it had to be endured.

Off-stage, John was a fascinating man. Kind and generous, he often took company newcomers under his wing and befriended them. He could be hilariously funny; he was artistic and liked making things; he liked painting; he enjoyed a whisky after a show; he loved cooking at home and, with his keen eye for fashion, was not unknown to make his own clothes. He was a loyal and caring friend. At work, he was a model professional who was generous in sharing the stage. He knew that his own successful characterisations were dependent upon the performers working with him and never took them for granted. When understudies went on, he was always available to run scenes and help them make the best of their opportunity because, if they did well, so did he.

But John, like many comedians, had his insecurities, which became increasingly obvious towards the end of his D'Oyly Carte career. It was always said that no star was bigger than the company and this proved to be John's nemesis. He was, by nature, a modest and unassuming man but, by the late 1970s, he seemed to have become increasingly unhappy and introverted, believing that the Savoy Hill management did not appreciate his value to the company. His work was never anything but the best he could give, but his mysterious falling out with long-standing friend and colleague, Kenneth Sandford, hinted at his increasing concerns about his status within the company. Ken never understood why John became so cool towards him, putting it down to something he must have said, but the rift in their relationship never healed.

It is true to say that John, more than any other principal, was used by the management to promote the company, leading to numerous press, radio and television interviews in his own time, particularly on overseas tours. His popularity with audiences made him a natural first choice to represent the D'Oyly Carte, but it was unpaid, extra work which he did not always feel he wanted to do if he was tired. Such publicity events meant having to travel to studios, paint on a smile and perform, often without thanks, because it was expected as part of his job. No wonder he felt taken for granted. After the North American tour of 1978, John was unhappy at the prospect of another long overseas tour the following year. He never liked flying and the idea of the lengthy journey to Australia was enough for him to tell the management that he did not want to go. However, the Australian promoters insisted that the tour would not go ahead without John Reed, so he was, eventually, persuaded, if certain conditions were met. His demands were, reluctantly, accepted by the management, but led to a complete breakdown of trust on both sides and John left the D'Oyly Carte at the end of that tour.

It was a sad end to a wonderful twenty-eight-year career with the company, but John had tired of his demanding job and was ready to embrace the opportunity to move on and meet other challenges. It is not difficult to imagine that he was in great demand as a performer and he particularly enjoyed his many trips to America. He also, occasionally, directed shows, but his new-found freedom meant that he had the welcome opportunity to spend more time at home after so many years on the road. However, he made a welcome return to the D'Oyly Carte, as a guest artist, for the company's final season at the Adelphi Theatre. His appearances delighted his fans but, more importantly, helped to smooth over some of the bad feeling associated with his departure from the company three years earlier: he was returned to the fold. Like all of us, John had his flaws, but he was a giant in his field, held in the greatest affection by fans and friends alike. He should be remembered as a talented, delightful man.

Will the D'Oyly Carte ever come back?

It already has, but as it was? No. However much we might like to romance that the iconic company could, one day, be brought back to life as it used to be, this remains an improbable dream. Theoretically, it is possible. The D'Oyly Carte Opera Trust is still active, but the scale of the operation required to tour several operas, both financially and logistically, makes this extremely unlikely. If we suppose that the trustees ever have the desire to resurrect the D'Oyly Carte as a full-time touring repertory company, have they the necessary resources to raise substantial capital; produce a sustainable business plan; employ appropriate artistic personnel to guide productions and trumpet all this in a blaze of publicity to ensure audience interest after long periods of inactivity? Unlikely, to say the least. They did bring the company back in 1988, playing a restricted repertoire that included operettas other then G&S, with limited success, but The New D'Oyly Carte never truly captured public interest in the same way as the original company and petered out a few years later. Despite high musical and performance values, its productions received mixed reviews, with enthusiasm for the return of company soon waning.

In recent years, the trust has lent the company name to Gilbert and Sullivan productions by Scottish Opera and, occasionally, staged operas under its own banner. With productions of *The Gondoliers* and *Utopia Limited* planned for 2020, the company name is far from forgotten but, however well-received these may prove to be, the D'Oyly Carte Opera Company is a very different animal these days. The success of the original company, for over a century, was due to its accessibility to so many people. It toured all over the UK and abroad, bringing as many of the G&S canon as possible to its loyal audiences. The present company does not do this, its performances limited to a handful of venues, thus restricting the number of people it reaches. What used to be staple fare in so many of our regional theatres is now only available to those who live within easy reach of London and the few touring dates the company undertakes. No longer seen by mass audiences, it is hardly surprising that interest in Gilbert and Sullivan has declined to such an alarming extent.

That people still ask if the D'Oyly Carte Opera Company might ever come back is an indication that its trustees and management have not been successful in raising public awareness that it is active. Die-hard G&S fans may know, but the many thousands of people who would enjoy seeing professional Gilbert and Sullivan in their local theatres have no idea that the company is still around. However much the original D'Oyly Carte was criticised for its 'old hat' productions toured on a shoestring budget, history shows it to have been a successful business operation for over a hundred years. So, what is better; touring cheap and cheerful productions of several of the Savoy Operas to a wide audience base, or putting large amounts of money into one or two high-quality shows seen by relatively few people every now and then? I think we can guess which way this will go. Maybe it is better to remember the original D'Oyly Carte with great affection than to wish for the impossible. It had its time.

CHAPTER EIGHT

AND THEN THERE WERE NONE

For those members of the original D'Oyly Carte still very much alive and kicking, it is a startling thought that, within the next two or three decades, there will be no-one left who appeared with the famous company. The youngest performer still alive is chorus soprano, Michelle Shipley, who somehow managed to talk her way into the company in 1979 at the tender age of sixteen. Still only fifty-seven years old, she is a mere babe by comparison with the rest of us. But, although creaking somewhat these days, we remain, in our heads, the young people who trod the boards week in and week out, travelled year-round and experienced the highs and lows of life on the road in the company of some truly remarkable people. That the famed D'Oyly Carte Opera Company was a unique and quirky theatrical institution is well-known, but it was the performers who made it so special. In both this book and my previous one about the company, personal stories bear witness to the larger-than-life characters, between 1950 and 1982, who were loved by audiences around the Gilbert and Sullivan world. It seems fitting to end with a few more tales about their experiences, even if, for obvious reasons, some must remain from nameless sources.

When Cynthia Morey joined the D'Oyly Carte in 1951, it was an ambition fulfilled. Loving every moment of company life, she quickly made friends, two of whom became life-long best buddies, John Reed and John Fryatt. Cynthia recalls that, although they had been close friends for a long time, John Fryatt was rather cagey about the fact that he had become follically-challenged and wore a hair piece. Intrigued by the fact that, although they had regularly worked together for many years, she had never seen him without his toupee, the wicked streak in her determined to catch him out. So, whilst he was staying with Cynthia and her husband, Tony, at their London home, she saw an opportunity by taking John an early cup of tea at a different time each morning. Knocking on his door, she took in the tea, convinced that he would be 'au naturel' but, whether it was earlier or later, he was always sat up in bed perfectly 'coiffed'. No sign of the toupee on the bed post, or put on slightly skewiff, he was always a picture of perruqial elegance. Much to her frustration, his dignity always remained intact and she still doesn't know how he did it.

Another life-long friendship between D'Oyly Carters was forged by the strangest of coincidences. It happened to Paul Waite, who spent four years with the company from 1973 as understudy to Kenneth Sandford. It's a fascinating story, as he explains.

'At the age of seven, I was sent to a tatty little boarding school for boys on the south coast. Some of the pupils were boarders, others were day boys who lived locally in Southbourne. One of these, Eddie, was a good pal of mine. He possessed a fine tenor voice and became a highly-skilled musician, although our headmaster, Mr Taggart, was very disparaging about his ambitions to become a professional musician. Well, he certainly got that badly wrong!

'In 1974, the re-gathering of the company after the summer break was, as always, a time of huge excitement and anticipation for everyone. This was when all the newcomers would meet the other members. As I stood looking across the rehearsal room at Sadler's Wells Theatre, I thought I recognised a familiar face. At first, I couldn't place him, but the penny soon dropped; it was my old school chum, Edwin "Eddie" Rolles, whom I hadn't seen for about eighteen years and there we were, in the same rehearsal studio, in the same company, staring at each other in disbelief. What an extraordinary coincidence it was!

'Eddie had acquired letters after his name from his studies at the Royal Northern College of Music, whilst I, on the other hand, had none, which made me feel slightly musically inferior and somewhat incomplete professionally. Eddie suggested that we could remedy this; he would get me through a musical diploma whilst we were on tour with the Carte. Having looked at various syllabuses, he decided that an ALCM was manageable in the time frame we had at our disposal. With Eddie's tuition, I sat the written paper in Sheffield whilst we were appearing in Yorkshire, then the practical performing part in London. Sure enough, with Eddie's help, I became a proud Associate of the London College of Music.

'I was later able to repay him in a small way when the dreaded annual "field day" came around. This was the nerve-racking event for choristers who wished to remain with the company, when they were required to re-audition on stage in front of the management. Eddie wasn't looking forward to this one little bit and asked if I could give him some tips on how to put over his song, which I duly did by giving him something to concentrate on during the audition. He succeeded in getting through for another year with no problem at all. We remained close friends throughout our time together in the company and have kept in contact ever since.'

Such a heart-warming story typifies the bonds formed in the D'Oyly Carte, where friends looked out for each other, but it was not unknown for some friendships to develop into something rather closer. Personal relationships between performers frequently occurred and were a source of companionship when out on a long tour. Many were openly carried out, but others were rather more clandestine; it was just the way it was and judgements were never made.

During the tour of Australia and New Zealand in 1979, one of Dame Bridget D'Oyly Carte's young ladies was involved with a fellow-performer and both wished to keep their association under wraps. However, they were almost rumbled one afternoon in Melbourne. An unexpected knock at the apartment door of said young lady led to her discovering the formidable figure of Beti Lloyd-Jones waiting to come in. As soon as the gentleman in question heard Beti's voice, he thought quickly and decided that his only option was to make an exit via the bedroom window (fortunately, it was a ground floor apartment!). As the two ladies chatted away in the lounge, he had no option but to crawl on his hands and knees through the rose bushes planted under the window which would have revealed his escape. Apart from a few scratches, he got away unscathed, but it was a close call. This escapade was, later that day, the source of much merriment for the two almost caught out. And how do I know about this? I'm sure you will have guessed.

An amusing incident no doubt, but it pales into insignificance when contrasted with the tale, told to me by Kenneth Sandford, about two D'Oyly Carte principal men seeing the same chorus lady without the other's knowledge. As I recall, it was the start of the annual holiday sometime in the late 1950s and the girl with two beaux to her string was waved off at the airport by one of them, to be met at her sunshine destination by the other. Those were the days.

A principal soprano with the company for two years from 1967, Susan Jackson's D'Oyly Carte career was short, but eventful, and she has many stories which still make her chuckle. Perhaps her favourite involved the company being invited to try the produce of a famous distillery near Edinburgh. As Susie remembers, it was a morning event but, although the golden spirit was served in thimble-sized glasses, it did not take too many of them for the effects of pre-lunch drinking to kick in. As she was playing 'Phyllis' in *Iolanthe* that evening, she refrained from temptation, as did most of the principals, but it was a different matter for the chorus.

'When I saw the fairies that night, I was astounded to see so many of them in disarray, with wigs askew and their trippings hither and thither decidedly off-kilter. I realised that they were still tiddly from sampling the different types of whisky earlier in the day. It was one of the funniest things I have ever seen. That is, if you don't count the time when our conductor, Jimmy Walker, fell off his podium in the middle of a show! Then there was the girl who met an American man during a tour of the States and married him within six weeks, only to find out some time later that he was a bigamist. I had been her bridesmaid and was the first to be told the shocking news. Life was never dull in the D'Oyly Carte.'

Overseas tours certainly provide many amusing tales of company members making merry during the months away from home. A particular company favourite from the 1976 American trip involved a chorus gentleman who got back to his hotel room late one evening after a show to inexplicably find a comatose chorus lady in his bed. Unable to wake her to find out how she got in and why she was there, in high dudgeon, he pulled the bed covers from her, drew the shower curtain and made himself as comfortable as possible in the bath tub. Awoken the following morning by the obvious sounds of someone using the toilet, the outrageous side of his nature kicked in and he could not resist throwing back the curtain to reveal himself in all his glory with a cheerful cry of, 'Morning!'. It is to be hoped that the horrified young lady learned her lesson.

One of the tricks to surviving long periods away on tour was to think of temporary accommodation as 'home', the private space providing sanctuary from work. As the days of theatrical landladies passed into history in the 1960s, many D'Oyly Carters chose self-catering flats, or houses, with cooking facilities to avoid the inconvenience and expense of eating out every day. Kenneth Sandford chose this option whenever possible and his way of making himself feel at home was to bake an apple pie big enough to last a week. As soon as he moved in, he got cracking, using the trusty pie tin he took everywhere with him. The limited range of kitchen utensils in most digs seldom included a rolling bin, but that was no handicap to chef Ken, who happily rolled out his pastry with a Coca Cola bottle. His other speciality dessert was pineapple upside down pudding, which, when all else failed, he would bake in a colander lined with aluminium foil. Needs must.

To keep down living costs, many company members chose to share accommodation and the camaraderie of living with colleagues spawned many an amusing story, although there were times when things were not always as they seemed. During a season in Bournemouth in the 1970s, a lady who had written to the company offering rooms in her home, on a self-catering basis, caused quite a stir when she marched into her kitchen and demanded to know what the hell two D'Oyly Carters thought they were doing. The reasonable response that they were cooking a meal did not wash with the furious landlady, who insisted that they immediately stop what they were doing and get out.

Having to look for somewhere else to stay was not the end of the matter, because the irate woman wrote to the Company Manager complaining that two of his performers had been found using her kitchen when she had specifically offered self-catering accommodation only. Obviously astonished by her inability to understand the term, he summoned the two choristers to his office to get their side of the story, but they need not have worried, because he wanted to reassure them that they were not in trouble, just unfortunate to have fallen victim to such a strange person.

Finding digs was always something of a lottery, with damp, or dirty, bedding an occasional problem and it was not unknown to be sharing with bed bugs, or to get body lice. Despite such hazards, most digs were adequate and good places were quickly re-booked for the next visit. Wishing to return to a house in Bristol, where a delightful elderly couple provided cosy bed-sits, James Conroy-Ward was disappointed to find they were all booked and that the attic, in which he had stayed once before, already had an occupant. However, it was suggested that, as there were two beds, he could share the room. It was not ideal, but very cheap, so James agreed. After all, the stranger should prove pleasant enough, but he got more than he bargained for on the first night, when his roommate assumed that James would welcome sharing one of the single beds!

Another story from Paul Waite, who always enjoyed being in accommodation with colleagues, details his efforts to do something nice for his flatmates, during a season in Torquay, which did not work out as planned.

'I was fishing off the harbour wall when my line got caught on the bottom, or so I thought. Whatever it was, it was darned heavy and my line was doubled over with the strain of hauling it up, so much that I thought it would snap. As it came closer to the surface, it revealed itself to be a massive crab, with huge claws and a very broad shell. I knew it was an edible variety, because I had seen them in fishmongers' windows. I eventually caught hold of the line and landed it by hand, still munching on my bait, on the wall.

'Our digs during the company's run at the Princess Theatre was a flat situated high up on a very steep hill overlooking the harbour, which I shared with others to keep down costs. I decided the crab was plenty big enough to feed us all, so I carried it all the way back up the hill. The girls were not too impressed with my idea of lunch and totally freaked out when the crab escaped from the bag it was in and started to explore the room. I told them that all they had to do was stick it in some boiling water and it would be done in a jiffy. In unison, the girls said they could not touch it, or do such a dreadful thing and I had to admit that I couldn't either; it would have been such cruel torture. In fact, nobody was going anywhere near it. There was only one thing to be done, so I took it all the way back down to the harbour to return it whence it came. I carefully dropped it back into the water and watched as it descended, its legs busily moving, so I knew it was unharmed by the experience, but with a hell of a tale to tell the nippers.'

Leisure time on tour was restricted to mornings when there were no rehearsals, or afternoons, if taking a rest before an evening performance was not seen as crucial. Sight-seeing, visiting art galleries, going to the cinema and playing golf were perennial favourites for Carte folk anxious to make the most of any free time they had. Lorraine 'Dulcie' Daniels, a principal mezzo-soprano in the latter years of the company, had never played golf, but her boyfriend at the time, tenor Barry Clark, had other ideas.

'Barry once bought me a set of golf clubs for my birthday. I used to play with Patricia Leonard and Barry with her husband, Mike Buchan. One day, I was about to take a shot when I noticed the men watching me from another hole. Trish kept me calm and gave me great encouragement, so I played the shot and it landed, in one stroke, near the hole. I can't tell you how pleased I was with myself, especially in front of the two men, both of whom were good golfers. The look on their faces said it all. We used to have such a laugh together. Sometimes, Trish and I went for spa days and I remember on one occasion, when we had been in the steam boxes, being told that we were then supposed to go naked into an ice pool. It was quite an experience; just use your imagination!'

Dulcie recently asked me if I could remember her favourite drink in D'Oyly Carte days. With the mists of time fogging my brain, I confessed I could not. She was happy to remind me.

'I hardly drank alcohol when I was with the Carte. With the exception of the occasional gin and tonic, my preferred drink was grapefruit and tonic. I named it a "Pinafore special". Hard to believe, but when I first met my husband, Brian, he also drank grapefruit and tonic. Now there was an omen. A drink that always reminds me of D'Oyly friends is bucks fizz, which was served with breakfast at the Savoy Hotel before our departure on an overseas tour. Nowadays, I have taken to enjoying Geoff Shovelton's favourite drink – a whisky mac.'

Not all performers were as abstemious as Dulcie. Drinking was always a part of D'Oyly Carte culture; it was a matter of finding a sensible balance for most people. A drink after the show was popular with many, but not to the point of excess. Pragmatism was the order of the day with the next day's show in mind and limited pocket money to spend. However, it was another matter if free booze was flowing at official receptions, or parties thrown by admirers of the company, when most drank more than was good for them. During the tour of Australia and New Zealand in 1979, the company's sponsor, Benson and Hedges, held a champagne reception after the opening night in every city we played, which everyone was expected to attend. At first, the glamour of quaffing several glasses of expensive fizz was delightful but, after a couple of these events, the attraction waned, the whispered comment of one chorus man summing up the feelings of many: 'What I wouldn't give for a pint of warm bitter.'

During the previous year's tour of North America, D'Oyly Carters were royally entertained by a wealthy fan of the company at his home on Cape Cod in Massachusetts. After fun on the beach and cocktails galore, it was on to a local clam house for a seafood supper. On the bus journey back to Boston, one of the chorus ladies threw up so often that she needed a couple of plastic bags, because it was not possible for the bus to keep stopping. Presumed to have had too much to drink, there was little sympathy for her. A few weeks later, a slap-up after-show party for the company was held at Washington's Mayflower Hotel, which saw a fleet of White House limousines convey the cast from the Kennedy Center Opera House. The same chorus lady again enjoyed a few cocktails and tucked into the seafood, but was so sick afterwards that she missed the performance the following day. The company manager was, understandably, not best pleased. Not usually known to drink to excess, her behaviour was out of character and it took a third incident before she worked out that eating shellfish washed down with spirits was the problem. Thereafter, she never mixed the two, but it took some time before her colleagues believed her! Remembering her embarrassment must be hard enough, so I will not name and shame her.

It was, of course, much easier for choristers to make the most of free time. Late night partying and going out for the day when they didn't have the responsibility of playing a principal role in the evening was a bonus, allowing them to enjoy local attractions to the full, particularly on an overseas tour, when sight-seeing was the order of the day. A final story from Paul Waite and his chum, Eddie Rolles, perfectly captures the carefree lives of choristers with time on their hands.

'While we were playing in Boston on the 1976 American tour, Eddie and I thought it was a great idea to explore rural Massachusetts, so we hired a car with three others and were soon off and away along the highway. I did the driving, as nobody else seemed keen to drive on the "wrong" side of the road. Very soon, I was driving very much faster than the 55mph blanket speed limit permitted in the state. We were merrily bowling along, chatting and singing, when out popped a State Trooper from behind a hedge. His dramatic gesticulations left me in no doubt that he wanted me to pull over, so I did as instructed and slowed down, to be confronted by another State Trooper waiting to collar me. I was very nervous and tried to look as crestfallen as Toad of Toad Hall when apprehended for speeding. My passengers, on the other hand, were thrilled to be pulled over by the law. As the immaculately dressed trooper, complete with broad-brimmed hat approached, I opened the window and listened very carefully to his reprimand, preparing to express regret for my reckless actions.

'He asked where we had come from and where we were heading. As soon as he heard my British accent and learned that we were all singers with a touring opera company from England enjoying exploring West Massachusetts, his whole demeanour changed and I think he would have given us a police escort if he could! In fact, the two troopers seemed delighted to have pulled up a bunch of opera singers from Old England. It was certainly a lucky break. They did give me a speeding ticket, but said that, because our company was soon moving to another state, I need not worry about paying the fine as it would be out of their jurisdiction! So we continued on our happy way and I caught a trout in a boulder-strewn river, whilst the others visited a small town. Back in Boston later that day, we fried up the trout and divided it five ways. It was one of the best days ever.'

Not all happy D'Oyly Carte memories sprang from such adventures; something as simple as a first meeting could leave an indelible impression, as Vera Ryan remembers only too well.

'When I joined the company in 1959, I was a well-sheltered Catholic girl from Manchester. Musically intelligent, yes, but worldly-wise, absolutely not. My first rehearsal was *The Gondoliers* at the Scala Theatre just off London's Tottenham Court Road. The whole company was there, with Isidore Godfrey at the helm, when I walked in with my best pal, Eileen Bruckshaw. Experienced choristers did their weighing up of us and the glamour boy of the principals, Alan Styler, leaning nonchalantly on a counter in the corner, did his weighing up of the new talent! The die was cast then and there. I married him within two years.

'At the first rehearsal break, Fred Sinden sat down next to me and introduced himself as Tom Round's understudy. I was new to the whole hierarchy and did not know Tom Round from Tom Cobley, so I was unimpressed, but I was impressed by Fred's thoughtful welcome. His wife, too, Beryl 'Tumpy' Dixon, was there. She was a lovely performer and I remember her singing 'The Oak and the Ash' at a golf club do. She is from the North East and those first words were so poignant to us Northerners far away from home: 'A North Country lass who to London had strayed'. As she sang the last line, she raised her glass and reduced us to tears.'

That Vera conjures up such vivid images of her first day in the D'Oyly Carte, some sixty years after the event, is a measure of the impact it had on the rest of her life. Although her company career was brief, choosing to leave after two years to raise a family, she is still a true D'Oyly Carter to this day. The happiness she found with Alan Styler shines through her words; is it any wonder that she fondly remembers their first encounter in such detail?

Working for the D'Oyly Carte always brought its fair share of hardship, so larger-than-life characters, who brought fun to the tedium of performing the same shows so many times, were a boon. One such was long-serving chorister and small part player, Jon 'Elli' Ellison, who first joined the company in 1953. He was a consummate professional and an excellent character actor, who brought definition to every role he played. An expert in make-up technique, Jon was always happy to help colleagues less adept in the art of applying 'slap', as it was fondly known. Solid and reliable, it is hard to imagine this pint-sized performer doing anything outrageous, but he was a master of mayhem, often reducing colleagues to hysteria with his subtle antics on the stage and bawdy pranks behind the scenes. As 'Bunthorne's Solicitor' in *Patience*, he would wander around the stage selling tickets to the aesthetic ladies hoping to win 'Reginald Bunthorne' in a raffle, every inch the crusty old lawyer. But his wicked asides to each lady were, for them, the highlight of the show. Invariably of a somewhat suggestive nature, his offers for them to possess his body were hilarious, but he never came out of character. Absolute genius!

In the men's dressing room, Jon could often be heard provoking gales of laughter with his cheerful vulgarity but, if truth is told, it was all for the entertainment of his colleagues. His real nature was that of an old-fashioned gentleman, who would never fail to doff his trilby whenever he met one of the company ladies. Always the first to offer to make sure any lady in accommodation on her own got safely into their digs after a show, he would accompany them, taking care to walk closest to the road. Jon was, and still is, a D'Oyly Carte legend. Quite right, too.

Another great entertainer of the D'Oyly Carte was principal tenor, Meston Reid, who joined in 1974, remaining until the company closed. Not of the same ebullient style as Elli, he was a wonderful raconteur, who could reduce his listeners to tears of laughter with his drawn-out shaggy dog stories and tales of theatrical mishaps. Delivered in a soft Aberdonian accent, his stories were a staple at company parties, requested time and again because he made them so funny. Reluctant to keep on telling the same old yarns, once persuaded, he somehow made them as fresh as on first hearing and we would laugh until our sides ached, even though we knew what was coming. His legendary telling of the story about the landlady who lost the Sunday joint of meat never failed to delight. An enormously popular character, his unexpected death, at the age of forty-eight, left his Carte colleagues in shock and disbelief that such a nice man had gone.

A contemporary and good friend of Meston was another great off-stage entertainer, James Conroy-Ward. As understudy and eventual successor to the great principal comedian, John Reed, James was used to the difficult task of deputising for his idol, sometimes having to contend with raw hostility from fans disappointed not to see John. It is difficult to imagine how he managed to perform under such conditions, but manage he did. It is interesting that when playing the 'Major-General', in *The Pirates of Penzance*, in which John did not appear, fans loved his portrayal and he never felt the same resentment; the pressure was off and he was able to make the most of those performances.

Although a nervous man by nature, James was a born comedian who loved nothing better than to make his colleagues laugh. A brilliant mimic, he was famous for his uncannily accurate impersonation of the company's General Manager, Frederic Lloyd. Capturing his physical mannerisms and voice to perfection, if overheard, James could easily have been mistaken for Mr Lloyd. Complete with monocle and heavy limp, everyone in the company laughed in delight whenever he took off the boss. In fact, he sometimes impersonated Mr Lloyd whilst talking to the man himself, much to the General Manager's amusement, who would chuckle when so outrageously confronted by himself. How he got away with it, we will never know.

Perhaps one of my all-time favourite recollections from my time with the D'Oyly Carte came courtesy of James. Whilst playing a rare season in Torquay, sometime in the 1970s, several of us booked into the same hotel, which had reception areas where we could relax after a show. In fact, I recall it had a ballroom with an electric organ, which we used for a noisy get-together late one night. Never much of a drinker, James ordered a couple of pints of Guinness from the bar one evening and then disappeared; to bed, or so we assumed. Within a few minutes he was back, dressed as his alter ego, 'Mrs Bagwash'. With a headscarf tied as a turban, a borrowed nylon overall, cigarette dangling from the corner of his mouth and leaning on a broom, he delivered an improvised monologue lasting some twenty minutes or so, in which he regaled us with the tales of woe befalling a landlady at the hands of her theatrical guests. Not only was his impromptu performance astounding, it was riotously funny; character acting at its very best. And all to entertain us after a show. What a shame the company's closure robbed him of the time needed to prove his innate comedy talents beyond any doubt.

Both James and Meston took something of a beating from Director of Productions, Leonard Osborn, during his tenure in the late 1970s. Never satisfied with their performances, his constant criticism of their work undermined the confidence of both men. In order to survive, they took delight in poking fun at Mr Osborn by doing impressions of him. James, of course, was brilliant at this, but Meston was a close second. Often, when sharing a dressing room, the two men would conduct their conversations in the manner of Mr Osborn and entertain their colleagues by addressing them in the same way. Meston was not unknown to put his nose in the air and ask in an aloof voice, 'Do you have a cigarette I can borrow?', which was one of Leonard's favourite ploys. Such behaviour may seem disrespectful and juvenile, but the Director of Productions was not held in high esteem; his bullying tactics upset too many performers for him to be popular. It is a pity that a star performer, a true matinee idol with audiences of the 1940s and '50s, should become a figure of ridicule in the D'Oyly Carte, but so it was.

We have seen that company members had many ways of spending the free time their busy schedules permitted, but a voluntary dance class? Surprisingly, when tenor chorister and company choreographer, Alan Spencer, broached the idea around 1977, it was received with enthusiasm. Meeting once a week in the ballet room at the top of Sadler's Wells Theatre during a London season, a dozen or so chorus members were joined by Ken Sandford to be put through their paces. Learning basic ballet, tap and modern dance techniques was seen as a great way to keep fit whilst improving stagecraft. Although a few fell by the wayside, most members of the group kept up the classes which continued when out on tour. In 1978, Alan made sure that his pupils had somewhere to practice in every city of the American tour, leading to a performance at the end-of-tour party in Boston. Cheered to the rafters by their impressed Carte colleagues, the dance group grew in confidence and continued through the following year, which included the tour of Australia and New Zealand. For those who invested in leotards, tights and ballet pumps, the rewards were great. All of us improved our dancing skills and enjoyed ourselves along the way.

But that was not where it ended. The development of the traditional Last Night of a London season from the sedate affairs of the 1950s to the wonderfully inventive romps of the late 1970s, provided a platform for Alan Spencer's trusty hoofers to shine. A well-known official company photograph, taken around 1955, shows D'Oyly Carters taking their calls at the end of a Last Night performance. On the set of *Trial by Jury*, with flats from *Patience* downstage, the jury box and public gallery were filled with characters from all of the operas, which was about as far as it went in terms of doing something different. Through the next two decades, Last Nights gradually became more adventurous, allowing the cast to let rip in style. Even at the end of the 1976 American tour, the management decided to give a Last Night performance, which saw Patricia Leonard dressed as the Statue of Liberty, John Reed as Uncle Sam, Kenneth Sandford as a lifeguard, complete with snorkel, and Michael Rayner as an American cop. The show may have mystified the American audience, but we had a grand time.

The final few London seasons played by the company saw Alan Spencer team up with Music Assistant, Paul Seeley, to produce some memorable Last Night routines featuring his dance class. Paul's skills as an arranger were given full rein as he came up with a rock version of 'The Magnet and the Churn' from *Patience*, with Ken Sandford as John Travolta and Trish Leonard as Olivia Newton-John, and a swing band version of the peers' chorus from *Iolanthe*. The latter saw the dance class girls in yankee sailor outfits tap dancing as the 'sailor peers' behind them played tambourines. Another number from *Patience*, "I cannot tell what this love may be", featured principal soprano, Barbara Lilley, joining the dancers for a comedy routine dressed as char ladies. Such departures from usual D'Oyly Carte performances were received with wild enthusiasm by audiences but, surely, it was those of us on the stage and in the orchestra pit who had the most fun.

For all the creativity of those latter-day Last Nights, a clear favourite for me was my very first in 1972, when John Ayldon made his appearance as 'The Mikado' astride a white horse which promptly deposited an unrehearsed mound in the middle of the stage. Never since have I heard so much hysterical laughter in a theatre. Hardly sophisticated humour, but the sight of 'Nanki-Poo' and 'Pish-Tush' clearing up the mess with bucket and spade was unbelievably funny, a moment never to be forgotten for cast and audience alike. The very last Last Night, in 1982, could not have provided a greater contrast, with tears of sorrow replacing tears of laughter.

To quote 'Ludwig' in *The Grand Duke*: 'Depressing subjects we'll not touch upon'. The D'Oyly Carte Opera Company, despite its sad end, had a proud heritage of bringing laughter and pleasure to audiences for one hundred and seven years. What other family-run British theatre company can boast such a successful history? Given that a Victorian composer and librettist created the masterful Savoy Operas as a means of making a fast buck for themselves and the impresario who spotted a business opportunity in bringing them together, it is easy to imagine they would never have believed it possible that their creations would still be popular around the English-speaking world in the twenty-first century. Handed such unique material, several generations of artistes breathed life into the characters and satire that started out as jottings on a piece of paper. They relished singing the music loved by so many and were privileged to bring the Gilbert and Sullivan operettas to audiences which never tired of seeing them.

W.S. Gilbert, Sir Arthur Sullivan and Richard D'Oyly Carte left a unique legacy for which we are truly indebted to them. They brought into being timeless works of genius portrayed for over a century by the many wonderful performers who were prepared to endure, in their service, the hardships of life lived permanently on the road. There may not be many of us left to remember both the good times and the bad, but we still have passion for our days on the D'Oyly Carte stage. I leave you with the words of Vera Ryan.

'Even now, after sixty years, I feel the thrill when any of the G&S overtures are played on the radio. Not often enough, though. There is still some disdain from the musical intelligentsia, who do not appreciate what they are missing. We do, don't we?'

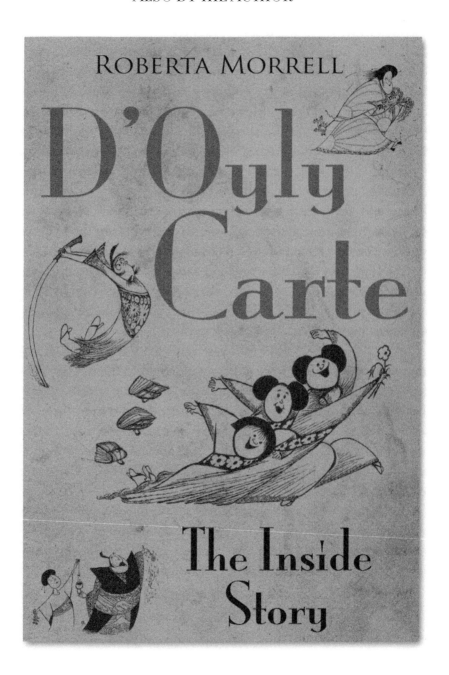

ROBERTA MORRELL

D'Oyly Carte

The Inside Story

 Matador